PRICE GUIDE TO

Coca-Cola

TRADE MARK ®

COLLECTIBLES

Wallace-Homestead

PRICE GUIDE TO

Coca-Cola

TRADE MARK ®

COLLECTIBLES

Deborah Goldstein Hill

Cover photograph: Arthur Hill

Library of Congress
Catalog Card Number 82-62060

ISBN 0-87069-378-6

10 9 8 7 6

Published by

Wallace-Homestead Book Co.
201 King of Prussia Road
Radnor, PA 19089

Contents

To my father, Sheldon Goldstein, for his dedicated commitment to gathering the finest collection of Coca-Cola memorabilia in the world. For over a decade, he spent the better part of every day corresponding with collectors. It was his devotion and excitement that stimulated the widespread interest in the field of Coke collectibles.

Acknowledgments

First, I would like to thank my husband, Arthur. It was his confidence in me that encouraged the undertaking of this project. He was forever supportive, guiding me through every step in preparing this book, including taking the photograph for the cover. To Arthur, all my love.

A special thanks to the rest of my family, too, including my mother, Helen, and my sisters, Jenifer, Lisa, and Ele Ann.

Thanks also to Peter Holden, who helped prepare the history section. His ability to condense large volumes of material accurately in a short time enabled me to meet my deadline. I would also like to thank Alan Baer and the staff at Calamity Jane's and Sam's Town for their hospitality, to all of the people from the Cola Clan who have made the last four years so pleasurable, to Steven Howard for his special care in reading and editing the manuscript, to Bob Anderson and Alison Frankley, my two best friends, who showed continuing support, to Gail Fakes, mostly for her love and interest, but also for her suggestion that I get a computer before I start this book, and to my neighbors, Scott, Jim, and Michelle, for their constant interruptions.

Finally, thanks also to the Coca-Cola Company, for seventy-five years of great advertising. I would also like to recognize Phil Mooney, Archives, Coca-Cola Company, Atlanta, Georgia, the many Coca-Cola bottlers across the country who have sent me information, Bob Buffaloe, the founder of the Cola Clan, and Sally Lorey and Alice Fisher for their contributions.

To the contributors of the Cola Clan's publication, *The Cola Call,* and to Cecil Munsey, for his work in the field of Coke memorabilia, a special thank-you. And, finally, special thanks to Candy Skinner.

Introduction

Certainly Coca-Cola advertising memorabilia is the most widely collected of all advertising collectibles. And it's little wonder when you consider the monumental quantity of items produced. Only Coca-Cola advertising memorabilia provides such an entertaining and idealistic panorama of American history.

I've often wondered how it would be to live in a time when a Coca-Cola cost only a nickel, when gas cost less than twenty-five cents a gallon, and a trip to the soda fountain was the main event of the day. It is a different world now. Ice-cold Coke now pops out of a talking vending machine that requires two quarters, and real soda fountains have become a rarity.

People will collect almost anything full of memories — baseball cards, bottle caps, or old dolls. My husband collects old cameras. Others may prefer political buttons, bottles, stamps, or coins.

This book has been prepared especially for those wonderful collectors who have been bitten by the "bug" for Coca-Cola collecting, or would like to be. It represents a century's worth of memories from the world's largest soft drink company.

Enjoy!

The creation of the most famous soft drink

In the spring of 1886, John Styth Pemberton was cooking up the first batch of what was to become Coca-Cola. Mixing the syrup in a three-legged iron kettle in the back yard of his Atlanta, Georgia, home, Pemberton experimented with what he foresaw as a headache remedy and "tonic stimulant." Clearly, John Pemberton could have had no idea that his formula would become the base of the most popular soft drink in the world.

Born in 1833, John Pemberton grew up and was educated in Columbus, Ohio. Part of his education consisted of an apprenticeship in pharmaceuticals. After the Civil War, Pemberton moved to Atlanta where he established himself as a druggist and pharmaceutical chemist. He became known for his original compounds advertised as health supplements and cures for various common ailments. Indeed, the precursor to Coca-Cola was a mixture designed to cure headaches. Pemberton patented this mixture in 1885 and called it French Wine Coca. By taking out the wine and adding a pinch of caffeine, extract of cola, and other ingredients, Pemberton formulated an as yet unnamed syrup, eventually the base of the now-famous Coke.

Shortly after its creation in May of 1886, Pemberton took a jug of his new syrup to Willis Venable, the manager of the largest soda fountain in Atlanta. Venable liked the taste when he mixed the syrup with water and agreed to sell the drink at his soda fountain.

A few months later, the story has it, a new soda clerk accidentally mixed the syrup with soda water. Thus, Coca-Cola as we know it was born. The name Coca-Cola was given to the drink after its popularity had grown and was chosen because it was an appealing alliterative combination of two of the drink's ingredients. Although ill health soon forced Pemberton to sell the rights to his new product, the special blend of ingredients basically has remained unchanged. Pemberton died in August of 1888 without seeing the complete success of his creation, but it is certain that he knew something of the value of the drink he had first made in a three-legged iron kettle two years earlier.

Turning great taste into an empire

On August 30, 1888, two weeks after the death of John S. Pemberton, Asa Griggs Candler acquired the remaining one-third of Coca-Cola stock for a mere one thousand dollars. Candler had become the controlling owner in the months prior to Pemberton's death and these final shares made him Coca-Cola's sole proprietor. Candler had spent a total of $2,300 on the rights to the soft drink that he would soon lead from obscurity to national prominence.

Asa Candler was born on December 30, 1851, near Villa Rica, Georgia. Although the Civil War had disrupted his education and had left him with only seven years of formal schooling, Candler became an apprentice to two doctors when he was nineteen years old. While he was unable to achieve his dream of becoming a doctor, Candler was able to amass a working knowledge of pharmaceuticals. In 1873, he moved to Atlanta where he was able to put this knowledge to work at the Pemberton-Pulliam Drug Store.

After building up a reputation and some capital, Candler and a partner started their own retail and wholesale drug business. The business suffered when their building was destroyed by fire. They purchased Pemberton, Iverson, and Denison, a drug company with which they could service their accounts.

Soon Candler became the sole owner of the company, and in August of 1888, he acquired the exclusive rights to Coca-Cola. Realizing its potential, Candler dropped all of his other products in order to concentrate on the soft drink. The decision proved to be a profitable one, as the company showed a $100,000 gross profit each of its first two years.

In 1892, Candler incorporated. He sold an initial 500 shares for $100 apiece. If you had been lucky enough to have acquired one of Candler's original shares of stock for $100, that same share would have been worth $17,000 in 1914.

In succeeding years, the Coca-Cola Company expanded enormously. Branch offices were opened in Dallas, Chicago, and Los Angeles. In 1909, the Atlanta operation moved into a huge, new building at the corner of Marietta and Magnolia Streets.

Candler stepped down as president of the company in 1916. It is obvious that his strength and dedication started Coca-Cola on its path toward success. During his reign, the Coca-Cola Company became one of the most successful businesses in the country.

Let's bottle it!

In the first years of Coca-Cola's existence, the popular beverage could be found only at the local soda fountain. It was not until the summer of 1894 that Joseph Biedenharn began to bottle Coke, the soft drink that was selling so well in his Vicksburg, Mississippi, store.

Biedenharn, a native of Vicksburg, was born December 13, 1866. As a teenager, Biedenharn joined his father's firm, which sold fruits, nuts, and candies. Eventually, he took over the company and moved it into a large building in Vicksburg. The success of his business allowed him to run both a retail candy shop-soda fountain as well as a wholesale candy and nut warehouse. In 1890, a Coca-Cola salesman persuaded Biedenharn to offer Coke at his soda fountain.

The Biedenharn Candy Company began bottling soda water in 1891, and three years later, introduced Coke by the bottle. The idea behind this innovation was to make Coke available to people who did not live near soda fountains.

The original Coke bottle had a six-ounce capacity and cost seventy cents for a case wholesale (compared to sixty cents for a case of regular soda water). Soon Biedenharn was delivering bottled Coca-Cola throughout the Vicksburg area and by boat up and down the Mississippi River. When he died in 1952, Joseph Biedenharn had been a Coca-Cola bottler for fifty-eight years.

Coca-Cola bottles

Since Coca-Cola was not originally created to be sold as a bottled soft drink, the founders could not have perceived the enormous potential in bottling their beverage.

Biedenharn was already bottling other drinks when he began bottling Coke. Bottles were used interchangeably, so the first Coke bottles did not bear the drink's distinctive logo. The short, six-ounce bottles used the popular Hutchinson stopper. This type of bottle top was rather bulky and consisted of a rubber gasket held between two metal plates attached to a spring wire stem. The bottles were identified only by the embossments "Registered" and "Biedenharn Candy Co., Vicksburg, Miss."

One of the central problems in the bottling industry before the turn of the century was finding a suitable bottle closure. There were hundreds invented during this period, including the Hutchinson stopper, but none was completely without problems. The main objection to the Hutchinson top was the fact that its rubber gasket became odorous and unsanitary if the bottle were not opened in about two weeks.

In 1891, William Painter of Baltimore, Maryland, invented what was to become the most practical and popular bottle top of the first half of the twentieth century — the crown cork. Although Coca-Cola did not make the crown cork mandatory with its bottlers until the emergence of its standardized bottle in 1916, this bottle closure marked an era of new sophistication in the bottling industry.

From "Deliciously Refreshing" to "Coke Is It" in seventy-five years

"The Pause That Refreshes." "It's the Real Thing!" "Things Go Better with Coke!" By the immediate familiarity of these phrases, it is clear that the promotion and advertising of Coca-Cola has been enormously successful. And, although John Styth Pemberton's syrup makes an undeniably great beverage, quality advertising has been a major force in turning Coca-Cola into the world's most popular soft drink. This success can be attributed in part to the continuity of the advertising principles initiated over seventy-five years ago by Asa Candler and W. C. D'Arcy.

Since the first Coca-Cola advertisements of the 1880s and 1890s, beautiful and elegant men and women have been shown in settings that the public admires and aspires toward. In its advertising, the Coca-Cola Company has presented itself as standing for quality, decency, wholesomeness, and, most important, the American way of life. Coca-Cola has always strived to align itself with the goodness of America and its people.

These principles are clearly seen even in the first lithographs of pretty, wholesome girls drinking Coke from Asa Candler's era. By the turn of the century, however, that medium was becoming obsolete and four-color advertisements were present in magazines. At that point, Candler decided to hand the growing task of representation over to the Massengale Advertising firm.

Massengale took over in the early 1900s, but their tenure was short-lived and their advertising pieces are now considered rare. In general, their advertisements showed beautiful people drinking Coke and playing what were then the sports of the rich — tennis, golf, and swimming.

In 1906, W. C. D'Arcy became Coca-Cola's advertising agency. Idea man Archie Lee and Coca-Cola President Robert Woodruff developed and produced ideas and copy that conveyed the image of clean Americana in the tradition that Asa Candler had begun. The look was generally the same, with wholesome and active men and women. The focus of the D'Arcy advertisements began to shift subtly towards the growing middle class. Their ideas were simple, always associating Coca-Cola with pleasant surroundings.

After Woodruff and Lee retired, the Coca-Cola Company changed advertising agencies. McKann-Ericson, which is still their advertising agency today, was chosen in 1956. The song, "I'd Like to Buy the World a Coke," was written by McKann-Ericson's Bill Backer. In the annual report of 1982, Coca-Cola states, "The Company's most successful advertising campaign ever developed for Coca-Cola — Coke is it! — achieved record consumer awareness."

In 1983, with over two million dollars in gross profits, the company introduced the most significant product addition in ninety-six years, Diet Coke — a collaboration of the world renown trademark with a great tasting, low-calorie soda. Given 100 more years and the great expansion of the low-cal market, we could see a book on Diet Coke memorabilia. It is the advertising of today that creates the memorabilia of tomorrow.

Starting a collection

Collecting Coca-Cola memorabilia allows a collector a great freedom for expansion and a wide variety of categories from which to choose. A collector may already have Coca-Cola items within his specialized collection. For example, there are many people who collect toys and trucks. Finding that they have several Coca-Cola items within their collections, they expand from there.

Other people like variety and collect every type of Coke memorabilia. We have everything from change trays and a pewter glass holder to a six-foot-long sign that hangs in my husband's studio.

There are also people who specialize in a particular category within Coca-Cola memorabilia. There is a man in Kentucky who has acquired over 100 different blotters during the last decade.

In the early 1960s, my parents began collecting Vienna art plates. My father was attracted by the beautiful women who adorned the plates. Western Coca-Cola Bottling Company was one of the many companies that used these art plates to promote their product. While vacationing in Solvang,

California, my parents ran across an ice cream parlor similar to Calamity Jane's in Las Vegas. My parents reminisced as they viewed the many serving trays displayed. It was then that they decided to build a collection of Coca-Cola serving trays.

They started searching antique stores, particularly those specializing in advertising antiques. They attended antique shows, auctions, and flea markets. They read and placed ads in the various trade papers. Of greatest significance, my father began to correspond daily with collectors around the world.

In the beginning stages of collecting, my father bought every item that was available. I think he feared that he would not see another. As he became more experienced, he began to upgrade his collection so that it included only items in mint condition.

By 1972, his was the largest and most complete collection of serving trays in the country, and it included two one-of-a-kind trays.

It was at this point that my parents began cataloging trays with the Coca-Cola girls known as Betty, Elaine, and Lillian. With the beautiful photographs and indexing completed, a book seemed a natural course. My parents introduced *Coca-Cola Collectibles, Volume I* in Indianapolis, Indiana, in 1972 at the first Advertising Antique Show. Because of the size and beauty of their collection, they were able to prepare a book each year after that. As the *Philadelphia Inquirer* of 1975 stated simply, "These books stimulated wider interest in collecting Coca-Cola items."

Photographs in this book were taken from these four volumes. Information about ordering can be found in the Source Directory.

Treasure hunting at swapmeets

If you are going to a swapmeet, go early. If you are a dealer with a booth, you usually have one hour to set up, so keep your display simple. As soon as you begin to unpack, you will find people roaming around to see what is around the next corner. Be ready. Much of the selling and trading is done before the doors ever open.

There is always a lot of activity at a swapmeet. Be careful about buying a questionable item. Use your book to identify the items and compare prices. Talk about your purchase with others; most dealers like to show their expertise.

There are always people who bring items to trade with the dealers. Sometimes they have an item that you have been wanting for a long time. This a good chance to make a great swap.

Swapmeets are exciting and there are so many opportunities to meet new friends. Buy anything that suits your fancy. As long as it displays the familiar trademark, it is collectible.

Auctions — "Going once!"

Auctions are fast-paced and high energy! I have brought home some true finds from auctions. I have also bought things that I wouldn't normally buy and possibly paid too much for certain items on occasion.

There is always an auction preview. This is where bidders have a chance to view the merchandise and note the identification number of the items they intend to bid on later. Once the auctioneer begins, however, it's time to pay attention.

Someone will show the item while you take a good look. Depending on the type of auction, the auctioneer will either ask for a bid or possibly start the bidding himself. Whether you are holding a number or a card, any motion to the auctioneer signals a bid. Depending on the item, bidding will start low with six to ten people bidding back and forth. As the price increases, a few will quietly bow out of the bidding. It usually ends up with two people bidding back and forth until finally one no longer bids. "Two-hundred fifty, going once, going twice, $250 going three times. Sold for $250." To you? Maybe. If it seems a little frightening, start by bidding very low, as close to the original bid as possible. On the fourth or fifth bid, sit back and you will be outbid. At least this will give you some practice. If you want the item, bid for it. Don't forget that payment is required at the close of the auction.

Dating by slogans

An advertising slogan is the easiest way to date an item. Because of the amount of standardization in relation to the advertising, most ads had the same look and offered the same messages. During any specific year, an advertising slogan would appear in almost all mediums — blotters, billboards, signs, newspaper and magazine advertisements. The following is a list of the slogans used in specific years.

1900
Deliciously refreshing
For headache and exhaustion, drink Coca-Cola

1904
Coca-Cola is a delightful, palatable, healthful beverage
Coca-Cola satisfies
Drink Coca-Cola in bottles — 5¢

1905
Drink a bottle of carbonated Coca-Cola
Coca-Cola revives and sustains
Drink Coca-Cola at soda fountains
The favorite drink for ladies when thirsty, weary, and despondent
Good all the way down
Flows from every fountain
Sold in bottles

1906
The drink of quality
Thirst quenching — delicious and refreshing

1907
Delicious Coca-Cola, sustains, refreshes, invigorates
Cooling . . . refreshing . . . delicious
Coca-Cola is full of vim, vigor and go — is a snappy drink
Sold everywhere — 5¢
Step into the nearest place and ask for a Coca-Cola
The great national drink

1908
Sparkling — harmless as water, and crisp as frost
The satisfactory beverage

1909
Delicious, wholesome, refreshing
Delicious, wholesome, thirst quenching
Drink delicious Coca-Cola
Whenever you see an arrow think of Coca-Cola

1910

Drink bottled Coca-Cola — so easily served

It satisfies

Quenches the thirst as nothing else can

1911

It's time to drink Coca-Cola

Real satisfaction in every glass

1912

Demand the genuine — refuse substitutes

1913

Ask for it by its full name — then you will get the genuine

The best beverage under the sun

It will satisfy you

A welcome addition to any party — anytime — anywhere

1914

Demand the genuine by full name

Exhilarating, refreshing

Nicknames encourage substitutions

Pure and wholesome

1915

The standard beverage

1916

It's fun to be thirsty when you can get a Coca-Cola

Just one glass will tell you

1917

Three million a day

The taste is the test of the Coca-Cola quality

There's a delicious freshness to the flavor of Coca-Cola

1919

Coca-Cola is a perfect answer to thirst that no imitation can satisfy

It satisfies thirst

Quality tells the difference

1920

Drink Coca-Cola with soda

The hit that saves the day

1922

Quenching thirst everywhere

Thirst knows no season

Thirst can't be denied

Thirst reminds you — drink Coca-Cola

1923

Refresh yourself

A perfect blend of pure products from nature

There's nothing like it when you're thirsty

1924

Pause and refresh yourself

1925

The sociable drink

Stop at the red sign and refresh yourself

1926

Thirst and taste for Coca-Cola are the same thing

Stop at the red sign

1927

Around the corner from anywhere

At the little red sign

1928

A pure drink of natural flavors

1929

The pause that refreshes

1930

Meet me at the soda fountain

1932

The drink that makes the pause refreshing

1933

Don't wear a tired, thirsty face

1934

Carry a smile back to work

Ice-cold Coca-Cola is everywhere else — it ought to be in your family refrigerator

When it's hard to get started, start with a Coca-Cola

1935

All trails lead to ice-cold Coca-Cola

The pause that brings friends together

1936

What refreshment ought to be

Get the feel of wholesome refreshment

1937

America's favorite moment

So easy to serve and so inexpensive

Stop for a pause . . . go refreshed

1938

Anytime is the right time to pause and refresh

At the red cooler

The best friend thirst ever had

Pure as sunlight

1939

Make lunch time refreshment time

Makes travel more pleasant

Thirst stops here

1940

The package that gets a welcome at home

Try it just once and you will know why

1941

A stop that belongs on your daily timetable

1942

The only thing like Coca-Cola is Coca-Cola itself

Refreshment that can't be duplicated

1943

That extra something

A taste all its own

1944

High sign of friendship

A moment on the sunnyside

1945

Whenever you hear "Have a Coke," you hear the voice of America

Happy moment of hospitality

Coke means Coca-Cola

1947

Serving Coca-Cola serves hospitality

Relax with the pause that refreshes

1948

Where there's Coca-Cola there's hospitality

Think of lunchtime as refreshment time

1949

Along the highway to anywhere

1950

Help yourself to refreshment

1951

Good food and Coca-Cola just
  naturally go together

1952

Coke follows thirst everywhere
The gift for thirst

1953

Dependable as sunrise

1954

For people on the go
Matchless flavor

1955

Almost everyone appreciates the
  best
America's preferred taste

1956

Feel the difference
Makes good things taste better

1957

Sign of good taste

1958

Refreshment the whole world
  prefers

1959

Cold, crisp taste that deeply satisfies
Make it a real meal

1960

Relax with Coke
Revive with Coke

1961

Coke and food — refreshing new
  feeling

1962

Enjoy that refreshing new feeling
Coca-Cola refreshes you best

1963

A chore's best friend
Things go better with Coke

1964

You'll go better refreshed

1965

Something more than a soft drink

1966

Coke . . . after Coke . . . after Coke

1989
You're the one — can't beat
*   th' feelin'.*

Grading condition

This guide to grading is the one established in 1965 by Sheldon Goldstein and has been unanimously used by collectors for almost two decades. Items can be classified and described in reference to their condition according to the following.

Special Rare Class. Items pre-1904 fall into this classification.

Mint. New condition. In original unused state. No visible marks.

Near-Mint. A classification into which most items that are thought of as mint would fall. Not in original mint condition. Close inspection would reveal very minor or slight marks of age or use.

Excellent. Only minor, hairline-type scratches visible without close examination. Small chip, chips, or marks on outer rim or edge of item.

Very Good. Minor surface scratch or scratches. Rust spots of no more than pinhead size. Minor flaking. Picture, lettering, and color in excellent condition.

Good. Minor scratch or scratches. Minor flaking. Minor fading. Possibly minor dents. Little rust or pitting.

Fair. Major scratch or scratches on surface. Picture or lettering faded. Rust spots on surface. Minor dent or dents. Bad chipping or flaking on surface.

Poor. Badly rusted, worn, dented, pitted, torn. Unrepairable.

Pricing

The most practical basis for pricing would seem to be what someone is willing to pay versus how much someone wants for an item. Without getting into the philosophy of sales, I can safely say that some Coke enthusiasts have no basis for what they are willing to pay.

While attending an auction several months ago I talked with a woman who has been working on her Coca-Cola toy collection for years. She had been searching for five years when she finally found the 1938 toy stove. I feel the basis for her purchase must have been what she was willing and able to afford versus how much the dealer needed to sell his treasure.

In *The Classic Collector*, spring 1974, my father was quoted as saying, "When I first started collecting Coke items eight years ago, people were complaining that the prices were too high. Five years from now, today's prices will look cheap in comparison." When my father finally did sell his collection, his playing cards sold for $50 to $100 a pack. Today these cards have sold at auctions for as much as $500.

Coca-Cola collectibles from A to Z

Blotters

Blotters were very popular in the first half of the century when dip pens and ink were used daily. Throughout the years, blotters have kept their basic oblong shape.

Slogan changes are significant as they depict the energy of the times. From 1927 to 1935, blotter artwork mimicked billboard artwork.

Set of six, 1920, **$300.**

Many collectible blotters can be identified simply by the phrase written across the front. Prices of the various blotters follow.

Blotter, 1904, **$50.**

Blotter, 1928, **$75.**

Blotter, 1929, **$30.**

Blotter, 1947, **$3.**

Bookmarks

Many Coca-Cola bookmarks are still in existence. People who are collecting books are frequently finding Coke bookmarks between the pages.

Hilda Clark, 1899, **$250.**

Hilda Clark, 1900, **$285.**

Hilda Clark, 1902, **$285.**

Lillian Nordica, 1903, 6″ × 2″, **$195.**

Lillian Russell, 1904, **$100.**

Coca-Cola Chewing Gum, 2″ × 6″,
1908, **$150.**

Owl, 1906, **$150.**

Books

The Romance of Coca-Cola, 1916.
Describes the history of Coca-Cola
through 1916, **$35.**

Alphabet Book of Coca-Cola, 1928,
$48.

Facts, 1923, **$30.**

The 5 Star Book, 1928, **$25.**

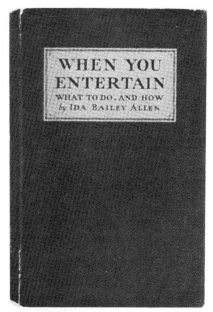

When You Entertain, 1932, **$12.**

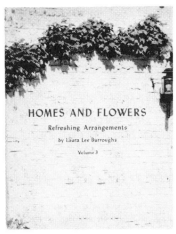

Home and Flowers, 1940, by Laura Burroughs, **$8.**

A Fascinating Hobby, Flower Arranging, 1940, **$8.**

The Red Barrel, 1940. These books, which were given to U.S. soldiers, kept our fighting men and women current of important news events, each **$8.**

My Daily Reminder, 1939, **$10.**

Our America, 1946. These books were distributed to schools, **$5.**

Know your War Planes, 1943, **$25.**

Easy Hospitality, 1957, **$5.**

The Coca-Cola Bottler, 1944, **$10.**

Pause for Living, 1961, **$20.**

Paper writing pad, 1960, **$7.**

Paper writing pad, 1950, **$7.**

Flags of the United Nations, 1960, **$5.**

Bottles

Here's how Coke bottles evolved over the years.

Hutchinson bottle, 1894, was the first bottle used by the Biedenharn Candy Company

Hutchinson bottle, 1899 to 1902, first bottle to be marked with the Coca-Cola script

Straight-sided bottle, 1900 to 1916, the first bottle to use the crown cork closure

Hobble skirt, 1915, designed by the Root Glass Company

Christmas bottle, 1923, the first universal design, was patented December 25, 1923

Christmas bottle, 1937, standardized in 1948 to hold 6½ ounces

ACL bottle, 1957, introduced the
first applied color label

No return bottle, 1961, was the first
one-way glass bottle. It was
later modified to include a twist
cap

Plastic bottle, 1975, is an experimental plastic bottle tested from
1970 to 1975

Biedenharn Candy Company, 1894,
$150.

| 1894 | 1899–1902 | 1900 – – – 1916 | 1915 | 1923 | 1937 | 1957 | 1961 | 1975 |

Nov. 16 — Dec. 25 — Aug. 3 (D-105529) — Applied Color Label (ACL) — One-Way Bottle (OWB) — One-Way Bottle (Plastic)

Chronology of the glass package for Coca-Cola 1894-1975.

Biedenharn bottle, 1900, **$100.**

Hutchinson bottle, 1902, **$250.**

Biedenharn candy, 1900, **$75.**

Syrup bottle, 1910. These bottles were given to drugstores for storing syrup to be mixed with seltzer, **$225.**

Coca-Cola syrup bottle, 1910, **$200.**

Coca-Cola syrup bottle, 1920, **$175.**

Drink Coca-Cola syrup bottle, 1910,
$210.

Drink Coca-Cola syrup bottle, 1920,
$100.

Christmas display bottle, 20″, 1923.
These bottles were full when on
display, **$125.**

Experimental plastic bottle, 1974.
Some of these are still found full, **$10.**

Hutchinson commemorative, 1961,
$100.

Syrup jug, 1930. Syrup was also
delivered in barrels, **$30.**

Older bottles can be dated fairly easily if you look for the series of manufacturer's numbers on the base or on the bottom of the bottle. For the number 18-30, for example, the first two digits (18) indicate the mold number. The second two (30) indicate the year of manufacture.

Presently, Coca-Cola bottlers code the four numbers somewhat differently. The first digit indicates the year; the second, the mold; the third, the manufacturer's symbol; and the fourth digit, the glass plant.

Another possibility for identification is bottle weight. The empty weights for Coca-Cola bottles get lighter each year (see the chart below).

Date	Empty weight ounces
1916 to 1936	14.24
1937 to 1956	14.01
1957 to 1958	13.80
1958 to 1962	13.65
1966 to present	13.26

Calendars

The first Coca-Cola calendar was issued in 1891. The first ten years displayed wholesome and pretty, but anonymous girls. As the company grew, they were able to engage the desirable actress Hilda Clark and the celebrated Metropolitan Opera star, Lillian Nordica, as models. After 1920, most calendars were released once again with unnamed models.

Many were printed in two versions, one with the model holding a Coke glass, the other, a Coke bottle. Since these calendars were distributed by bottlers, there are more calendars displaying bottles than glasses. Calendars with both renditions came out in the following years: 1903, 1904, 1914, 1915, 1916, 1917, 1919, 1920, 1923, and 1927.

It is very difficult to find a calendar complete with pad or all calendar pages intact. Without pad or pages, calendars cannot be considered in mint condition. They are still very beautiful and valuable, however.

The first Coca-Cola calendar printed by Calvert Lithography Company of Atlanta, Georgia, 1891, **$3,500.**

Calendar illustration without the pad, 1898, **$1,500.**

This calendar shows the first coupon offering a free Coca-Cola, 1897, **$2,500.**

In the same condition as the 1898 issue, 1899, **$1,500.**

Calendar for 1901, **$1,500.**

The model in this 1903 calendar holds the same glassholder used in the 1902 issue. Both calendars were printed by the same company, **$1,200-1,500.**

This photograph of Hilda Clark for the 1902 calendar was copyrighted in 1900 by Morrison of Chicago. The printing was done by Wolf and Company, Philadelphia, **$1,200-1,500.**

Lillian Nordica decorates both this 1904 issue and the 1905 version. This same calendar photograph exists elsewhere with one change — instead of the glass on the table, there is a bottle. **$950-1,050.**

Calendar for 1906, **$950-1,100.**

Good to the Last Drop, 1908 issue. Maxwell House later made this slogan famous with their coffee, **$900-1,000.**

Calendar for 1907, **$900-1,100.**

This 1909 calendar has the same photograph of Lillian Nordica that was used on the 1905 issue, **$650-950.**

This 1910 issue is a "top" only, **$500.**

This calendar, issued in 1912, is the first featuring two models, **$750-900.**

Coca-Cola girl calendar for 1910, **$950-1,200.**

Calendar for 1913, **$750-900.**

Betty was one of the most popular Coca-Cola girls ever. She appears on almost all of the advertising pieces of 1914, including this calendar. In 1970, a Betty calendar could be found for $100, **$500-550.**

The Knitting Girl, 1916, **$350-450.**

This 1915 calendar's value increases $300 if the model is pictured holding a bottle, **$500-550.**

World War I Girl, 1917, **$425-450.**

Also issued in 1917, **$425-450.**

Calendar for 1919, **$500-600.**

Calendar for 1918, **$500-750.**

The Garden Girl, 1920, **$350-400.**

Calendar for 1921, **$300-350.**

Calendar for 1923, **$225.**

The Autumn Girl, 1922, **$300-350.**

Calendar for 1924, **$225.**

Calendar for 1925, **$225.**

Calendar for 1926, **$225.**

Calendar for 1927, **$225.**

Calendar for 1928, **$225.**

The Bathing Beauty, 1930, **$400.**

Calendar for 1929, **$350.**

Farm Boy with Dog, painted by Norman Rockwell for 1931 issue, often called "Tom Sawyer" by collectors, **$350.**

Norman Rockwell 1932 calendar, affectionately referred to as "Huckleberry Finn," **$175.**

A Norman Rockwell 1934 issue, **$185.**

The Village Blacksmith by Frederic Stanley, 1933 issue, **$175.**

Norman Rockwell, 1935 issue, **$185.**

Artist N. C. Wyeth produced this 1936 issue, **$175.**

Created by Bradshaw Crandall, 1938, **$175.**

N. C. Wyeth, 1937 issue, **$175.**

Notice that the glass in the photograph for this calendar is un-marked, 1939, **$150.**

Calendars dated before 1940 are much harder to find. Luckily, Coca-Cola continued the practice of calendar advertising during the war years. Less expensive and more easily obtainable, the following calendars are very collectible.

The Pause That Refreshes,
1940 .... $125
Thirst Knows No Season,
1941 75
Thirst Knows No Season,
1942 50
Calendar honoring the U.S.
Army Nurses Corp, 1943   50
The Pause That Refreshes,
1944 50
Boy Scout calendar, Rock-
well art, 1945 150
Thirst Knows No Season,
1945 50
Boy Scout calendar, Rock-
well, art, 1946 150
Calendar for 1946 45
Girl with skis, 1947 45
Girl with a bottle, 1948 40
Girl with cap and boots,
1949 40
Hospitality in Your Hands,
1950 40
Entertain Your Thirst,
1951 40

Coke Adds Zest, 1952 45
Work Better Refreshed,
1953 40
Pause Refresh, 1954 35
Coke Time, 1955 30
Coke Time, 1956 25
The Pause That Refreshes,
1957 25
Sign of Good Taste, 1958 .. 25
Basketball game, 1959 20
Ski . . . Be Really Refreshed,
1960 20
Ski . . . Be Really Refreshed,
1961 15
Girl in front of mirror,
1963 15
Things Go Better with Coke,
1964 15
Things Go Better with
Coke, 1965 15
Things Go Better with
Coke, 1966 15
For the Taste You Never Get
Tired Of, 1967 15
Coke Has the Taste You
Never Get Tired Of, 1968   15

Cars and Trucks

Sprite Boy, 1945, **$100.**

Drink Coca-Cola in bottles, 1945, **$75.**

Coke truck, 1950, **$50.**

Buddy L truck, 1960, **$75.**

Open truck, 1950, **$75.**

Coke can car, 1972, **$20.**

Car, 1950, **$35.**

Semi truck, 1972, **$50.**

Bus, 1950, **$35.**

Truck, 1973, **$15.**

Cars and trucks not illustrated include:

Metalcraft truck, 1930, 11″,
rubber wheels $300

Metalcraft truck, 1930, with
working headlights...... 400

Budgie truck, 5″, yellow,
1950s 125

Early matchbook truck, 2¼″,
1950s 50

Enclosed truck, 1950s 45

Ford station wagon, 5″,
1950s 50

Marx truck, 1950s, cases and
bottles.............. 75

Marx truck, 1950s, cases,
bottles, miniature hand
truck.............. 75

Marx truck, plastic, 1950s,
Louis Marx & Company,
New York 125

Truck, 8″, 1950s 40

Bottle truck, 4½″, semi,
1960s 35

Buddy L, 1960s 40

Pickup, 1960s 90

Things Go Better with Coke,
4½″, 1960s 25

Truck, 2¾″, 1960s 30

Flatbed, 1½″, 1970 25

Roadster model, 1971 25

Eight-wheeler truck, 9½″,
1974 30

Modern logo truck, 1974 .. 25

Bus, double-decker, 3″,
1975 20

Cartons and bottle holders

Shipping case, 1906, **$175.**

Six-bottle holder, 1933, **$25.**

July Fourth wrapper, 1935, **$75.**

Six-bottle holder, 1937, **$35.**

Take-home carton   1939, **$25.**

Take-home cartons, 1940, **$20.**

Car window holder, 1940, **$30.**

Car bottle holder, 1950, **$25.**

Clocks

Baird Clock Company produced the first clock used to promote the Coca-Cola Company. Soda fountains that sold over one-hundred gallons a year were able to obtain a clock. The advertisement was embossed on the circular plaster of Paris frame.

The company later standardized their advertising message and promoted "Drink Coca-Cola" on all clocks.

The Gilbert Clocks from the 1920s have become easier to obtain. They are also easy to identify. Look for the sticker glued to the back, which states: "The Wm. L. Gilbert Clock Co., Winsted, Conn."

Baird clock, 1893, **$3,500.**

Baird clock, very rare, 1892, **$3,500.**

Desk clock, embossed bottles, 1907, **$450.**

Desk clock, 1907, **$400.**

Dome clock, 1910, **$500.**

Drink Coca-Cola, 40″ × 18″, 1909, **$1,500.**

Wall clock, 1915, **$800.**

Pocket watch, 1920, **$300.**

Reissue clock, 1972, **$40.**

Dome clock, two bottles, 1950, **$300.**

Reissue Betty clock, 1974, **$40.**

Coca-Cola chewing gum

While most people associate the familiar Coca-Cola trademark with the popular soda, the logo also has been used to represent other items. In 1908, the Franklin Manufacturing Company of Richmond, Virginia, produced a chicle that "aids digestion and gives comfort after a hearty meal."

Coca-Cola Pepsin Gum was introduced in a catalog by Schaack & Sons of Chicago. Twenty packages, five cents each, sold wholesale for sixty cents.

The glass Coca-Cola Chewing Gum roulette wheel shown on page 60 was displayed for many years on a drugstore counter in a small town in South Carolina. It is the size of a dinner plate and weighs three or four pounds. A marble rolls around the interior circumference of the wheel and drops into one of the numbered slots in the center. Children probably used the roulette wheel to win either a stick of gum or possibly a glass of Coke.

In 1980, an antique store merchant from South Carolina wrote after reading my monthly column in the *American Collector.* He had acquired this piece twenty years earlier when he purchased the estate of the woman who had once owned the above mentioned drugstore. He kept the roulette wheel for many years on his own counter. Although he had never intended to sell it, he explained that he needed money to put his son through college. He offered to sell it to me.

This roulette wheel has the second highest value of any chewing gum-related item. Because it is one-of-a-kind, I am very proud to have it in my collection.

My father discovered the very rare 1902 cylindrical gum dispenser illustrated here from a man who collected only chewing gum dispensers. When my father later sold it to the Schmidt Museum, this one-of-a-kind collectible brought top dollar.

Coca-Cola Gum, 1902, **$300.**

Cylindrical gum dispenser, 1902, **$5,000.**

Bookmark, 1904, "The Gum That's Pure Contains The Tonic Properties of Coca-Cola and Pure Pepsin." A book dealer ran across this very rare item in a book, **$375.**

Ad in *Everybody's Magazine,* 1904, **$35.** Similar ad in *Everybody's Magazine,* 1906, **$50.**

Gum package wrapper, 1906, Manufactured by the Franklin Caro Co., **$200.**

Shipping case, 1906, **$200.**

59

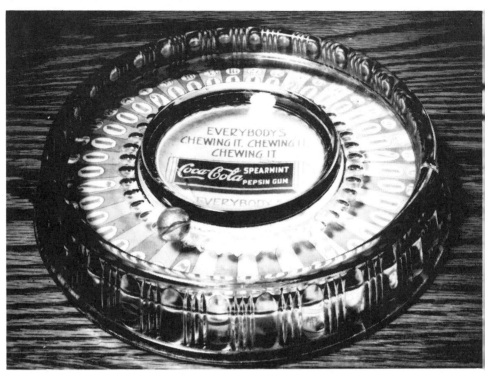

Glass roulette wheel, 1908, **$3,000.**

Coca-Cola Gum fan, 1910, front and
back. The front of the fan shows the
Franklin Caro Manufacturing Company, Richmond, Virginia, **$200.**

Gum display box, 1913, **$650.**

Apothecary jars, 1915. Coca-Cola
Pepsin Gum, **$600.** Coca-Cola
Chewing Gum, **$375.**

Gum display shipping box, 1913.
Placed in plastic for preservation,
$500.

Coca-Cola Gum paperweight, 1916,
$50.

Coolers and miniatures

Embossed bottles and cases, 1920.
The bottles are glass, **$45.**

Salesman's sample cooler, 10″ × 11″,
1934, **$375.**

Miniature glass perfume bottle, 1930,
$50.

Salesman's sample cooler, 10″ × 11″,
1934, **$375.**

Bottle ice cooler, 1934. Held block
ice to cool bottles, **$350.**

Miniature plastic bottle, 1951, **$5.**

Plastic dispenser, 1950, **$35.**

Miniature bottle lighter, 1950, **$10.**

Plastic dispenser, 1960, **$25.**

Plastic bottles and case, 1971, **$20.**

Miniature six pack, 1973, **$4.**

King and regular size bottles and case, 1971, **$25.**

Miniature six pack, gold metal, 1973, $

Plastic bottles and case, 1973, **$5.**

Coupons

Heart-shaped, 2″ × 2¼″, front and back, 1898, **$285.**

Celluloid, 1899, **$225.**

Hilda Clark, 3¾″ × 1½″, front and back, 1900, **$200.**

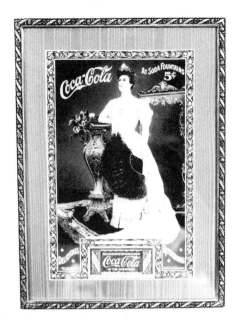

Lillian Russell, 1904, **$200.**

Delicious and Refreshing, 1904, **$50.**

Three coupons, 1905, each **$50.**

Coupon book, 1920, **$40.**

Golfer, 1928, **$40.**

Soda jerk, 1927, **$75.**

Take Home a Carton, 1939, **$10.**

Fans

These fans were given to stores and distributed to the customers.

Drive with Care, 1928, **$100.**

Quality Carries On, 1942, **$25.**   Drink Coca-Cola, 1950, **$20.**

Glass items and lamps

Syrup dispenser, 1895. The syrup has saturated the porous ceramic, **$3,000.**

Glass change receiver, Hilda Clark, 1900, **$1,000.**

Ceramic change receiver, 1900, made by Charles Lippincott & Company of Philadelphia, **$1,000.**

Milk glass shade, 1920, **$700.**

Glass change receiver, 7" dia., 1920, made by Wolf & Company, Lithographers, **$400.**

Leaded glass bottle, 36" high, 1920, **$3,500.**

Milk glass light fixture, 1920, marked on top band—"Property of the Coca-Cola Company. To be returned upon demand," **$1,500.**

Snack bowl, 1920, **$100.**

Lenox china plate, 10½″ dia., 1950, **$100.**

Leaded glass globe, 1928, **$5,000.**

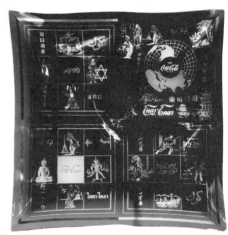

World dish, 11½″ × 11½″, 1967. Shows where Coca-Cola is sold around the world, **$50.**

China plate, 10½″ dia., 1930, **$100.**

Swedish glass plate, 8¼″ × 6¼″, 1969. Originally came in a felt bag, **$75.**

World dish, 7½″ dia., 1967, **$50.**

Glasses

Coca-Cola 5¢, 1900, **$200.**

Drink Coca-Cola, 1905, **$175.**

Pewter, 1930, **$150.**

Coca-Cola, 1935, **$35.**

Knives

Knife and corkscrew, brass, 1906, both sides shown, **$350.**

Switchblade, bone handle, 1908, **$75.**

Compliments the Coca-Cola Co., 1930, $75.

One blade, 1930, $75.

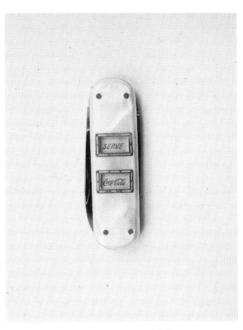

Serve Coca-Cola, 1950, $35.

Magazine advertising

Early advertising showed elaborately dressed people drinking Coca-Cola. The slogans always emphasized the popular Coca-Cola trademark. Advertisements for Coke appeared frequently in these publications: *The Housekeeper, Woman's Home Companion, Ladies' Home Journal, Redbook, Better Homes and Gardens, McCall's, Sports Illustrated, National Geographic, Motor Trend, Car Craft, Sports Car Graphic, Hot Rod, Boys Life, American Girl, Seventeen, Saturday Evening Post, Success, Literary Digest, Life, Delineator, Sunset, Pictorial Review,* and *Farm and Home.*

Two-color ads appeared on both the front and back covers of these publications: *The Housewife, The Household,* and *People's Popular Monthly.*

Miscellaneous

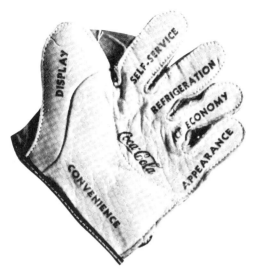

Comb, 1940, **$15.**

Baseball glove, 1927, **$300.**

Cowboy hat, 1974, **$175.**

Car key, 1950, **$35.**

Doorknob, 1920. Purchased from a man who bought some doors at an old hotel, **$275.**

Door lock, 1910. "Kam-Indore Lock Co.," also bottle opener, **$75.**

Door push (porcelain), 1930. Placed across the screen door at grocery stores so that customers couldn't put their hands through the screen, **$65.**

"A Float with a Coke" (plastic), 1945, container holds ice cream, **$15.**

Door push, 1950, very popular, **$75.**

Fountain seat, 1910, **$200.**

Golf tee set, 1950, **$15.**

License plate, 1950. Background is white with red lettering, **$25.**

License plate, 1950. Red background with white lettering, **$25.**

Keychain, 1955, **$35.**

Kit Carson poster, 1950, **$10.**

Krumkake maker, 1920, **$600.**

This and other similar hand-painted glass slides were used as commercials during intermission. Produced in St. Louis for one dollar. Other signs include "A Home Run," 1927, **$100**; "Good Company!" and "Unanimous Good Taste," 1928, each **$100**.

Magic lantern pictures, "Stop at the Red Sign," 1926, **$100**.

Needle case, 1924, **$50**.

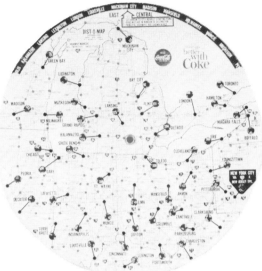

Mileage table, cardboard, 1950, **$40**.

Olympic record indicator, 1932. Souvenirs from the 1932 Olympics. Coca-Cola was a sponsor at the tenth games, **$35**.

Mileage and route information indicator, bright red, 1950. Gives distance from one location to another, **$200**.

77

Place mats, 1974, set **$15.**

Pillow, 1940, **$20.**

Pretzel dish, aluminum, 1936, **$40.**

Perfume bottle and holder, sterling silver, 1924. Inscribed "Top Hat Jewelry Company by Wells." The top flips open to the side and holds the dauber in place, **$250.**

Safety marker, 1900. Used at crosswalks, **$400.**

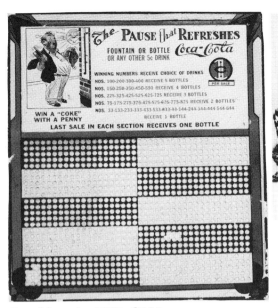

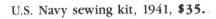

U.S. Navy sewing kit, 1941, **$35.**

Punchboards, 1929, **$200.**
Same price for the 1920 issue. People bought punches hoping to win three five-cent bottles of Coke.

Sugar rationing book, 1943, **$45.**

Token, 1930. A giveaway used as a slug to obtain a free Coke from a machine, **$10.**

Salt and pepper shakers, 1920, **$150.**

Thimble, aluminum, 1920, **$35.**

Planter sconce, 1920, **$150.**

Token holder, 1943. Used to hold O.P.A. rationing tokens, **$35.**

Other items not pictured, but equally collectible, include:

Binoculars, 1910 . . . . $200
Celluloid pencil holder,
   1910 100
Wooden bench, 1910, "Coca-
   Cola in bottles" written
   across the backrest 300
Commemorative fifty-dollar
   gold coin, 1915 75
Convention pin, 1916 150
Silverware, 1920 35
Driver's hat pin, 1930 40
Pencil box, 1930 30
Pencil sharpener, 1933 25
First aid kit, 1940 35
Ice pick and opener, 1940 10

U.S. Army sewing kit,
   1941 35
Baseball bat, 1950 125
Kit Carson handkerchief,
   1950 20
Pen, 1950 30
Bottle cap sharpener,
   1960 10
Hall of Fame records,
   1960 35
Service pins
Pledge pin 35
Five-year 45
Ten-year 55
Fifteen-year 75
Twenty-year 75
Thirty-year 100
Fifty-year 175

Newspaper advertising

The first newspaper advertisements were most often placed by individual bottlers. In 1906, the D'Arcy agency began standardizing advertising copy. Coca-Cola made many appeals to their distributors for uniformity. In 1926, just over one-half of all bottlers were using company-prepared advertisements.

In 1939, the Coca-Cola Company offered their bottlers a cooperative advertising program. Based on per capita consumption, the company assumed from 50 to 80 percent of all advertising costs. They also provided art for ads that bottlers could place in their local newspapers. For obvious reasons, this lessened the amount of individually created advertisements.

Newspaper advertisements are a pictorial representation of the history of both the Coca-Cola Company and the United States. A chronological collection of these slogans makes a very nice collection.

Openers

Opener, 1910, **$40.**

Bone-handled knife, 1908, **$100.**

Spoon opener, **$50.**

Opener, 1920, **$25.**

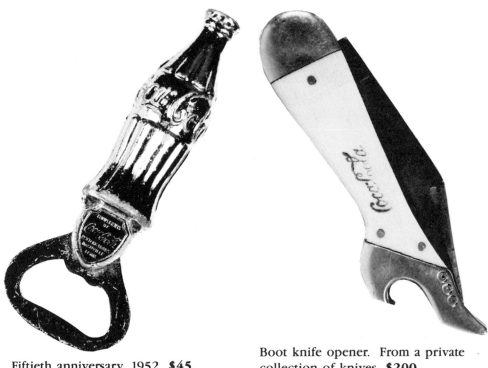

Fiftieth anniversary, 1952, **$45.**

Boot knife opener. From a private collection of knives, **$200.**

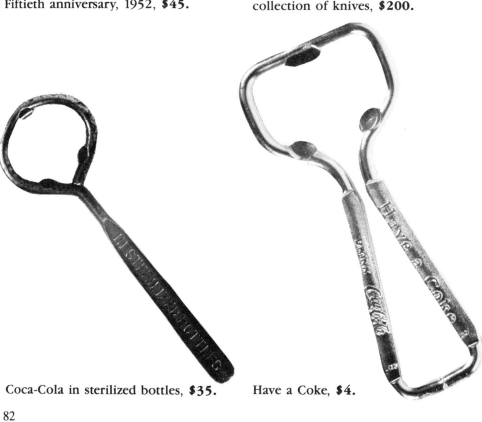

Coca-Cola in sterilized bottles, **$35.**

Have a Coke, **$4.**

Block print opener, **$35.**

Flat-shaped bottle opener, **$25.**

Oval-shaped bottle opener, **$35.**

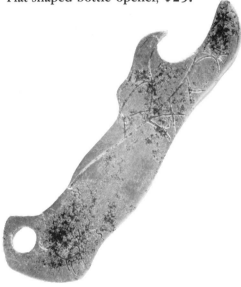

Skate key opener, **$35.**

Legs opener, **35.**

Drink Coca-Cola, **$10.**

Beer-type opener, **$8.**

Coca-Cola in bottles, **$15.**

Hilda Clark note pad, 1902, **$350.**

Paper Items

Celluloid postage stamp holder, 1901.
Stamps go in between the pages so
they don't stick together, **$400.**

Celluloid note pad, 1902, **$300.**

Trade card, folded and unfolded, 1905. Distributed by Western Coca-Cola Bottling, **$350.**

Opera program, 1906, **$45.**

Pocket secretary, 1920. Given to management within the bottling companies. There is a pen inside, **$75.**

Note pad, 1905, **$200.**

Book cover, 1925. Distributed to school bookstores to be given to book purchasers, **$10.**

Nature study cards, 1928, **$45.**

Bottle bags, 1932, **$5.**

Miniature ad, 1929, **$35.**

Souvenir money, 1931. Confederate
one-hundred dollar bill, **$40.**

Score pad, 1941, **$7.**

Playing cards

Plant tour gift, 1948, **$25.**

Cards, 1943, produced during a time when schools were having regular air raid drills. These were provided to schools to help teach children how to spot enemy planes, **$20.**

Book cover, 1951, **$5.**

Coca-Cola Relieves Fatigue girl, straight-sided bottle and straw, blue inset border, 1909, copyright by S. L. Whitten, Chicago, Illinois, **$500.**

Girl with a Parasol, 1915. Western Coca-Cola Bottling Company of Chicago, Illinois, offered these cards for twenty-five cents in stamps. The joker shows a straight-sided bottle with a paper label, **$350.**

The Ice Skater, 1956. Commemorates the seventieth anniversary of Coca-Cola, **$20.**

Girl with Bobbed Hair . . . Tastes Good, 1928. These cards have four different borders: red, light yellow, light gray, and red with gold edge, **$200.**

The Girl with a Bowling Ball, 1961, **$15.**

The Stewardess, 1943. During the war Coca-Cola distributed the double-deck bridge sets depicting the nurse and the switchboard operator. They sold for thirty-three cents to the bottlers, **$35.**

Boy and Girl at Fireplace, 1963, **$15.**

Additional sets not pictured include:

Pocket mirrors

Women frequently carried pocket mirrors because they could be stored conveniently in their purses. There are many reproductions, but they are easy to spot once you've seen an original.

Information shown in quotation marks is the copy as written on the bottom and side rim of the mirror. This is the easiest way to identify an original. Before 1913, all pocket mirrors came with the following copy: "Duplicate Mirrors 5¢ Postage, Coca-Cola Company, Atlanta, Ga."

Oval, "Bastian Bros. Co. Rochester, N.Y.," 1903, **$375.**

St. Louis, "J.B. Carroll Chicago," 1904, **$250.**

Juanita, "The Whitehead & Hoag Co., Newark, N.J.," 1905, **$250.**

Coca-Cola girl, "J.B. Carroll Chicago," 1909, **$200.**

Relieves Fatigue, "From the Painting Copyright 1906, by Wolf & Co. Phila. Bastian Bros. Co. Roch. N.Y.," 1906, **$250.**

Coca-Cola girl, "The Whitehead & Hoag Co. Newark, N.J.," 1911, **$200.**

Oval, 1914, **$250.**

Bathing suit girl, "The Whitehead & Hoag Co. Newark, N.J.," 1918. The hardest to find, only three are known to exist, **$350.**

Elaine, "The Whitehead & Hoag Co. Newark, N.J.," 1917, **$200.**

Garden girl, "Bastian Bros. Co. Rochester, N.Y.," 1920, **$250.**

Postcards

Duster girl, 5½″ × 3½″, 1906, **$350.**

Other postcards not illustrated:

Delivery wagon, 1900	$100
Bottling plant, 1904	100
Bottling plant, 1905	100
Bottling plant, 1906	100
Bottling plant, 1910	50

Delivery wagon, 1913, **$100.**

The Coca-Cola girl, 5½″ × 3½″, 1909, **$350.**

Delivery wagon, 1915, **$35.**

ALL OVER THE WORLD

You will find *Coca-Cola* signs that create a demand which you must supply. Don't miss the chance.

It's the sign of prosperity

All Over The World, 1913, **$100.**

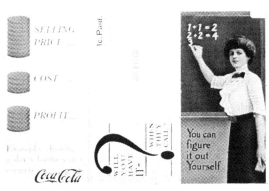

Foldout, 1913. This postcard came in five versions, **$85.**

Dick Tracy, 1942, **$125.**

Radio advertising

Many of Coca-Cola's first radio spots were recorded on disks that are widely traded and collected.

The Coca-Cola Company began its radio advertising in 1927 with a fourteen-week program about the romance between Vivian, the first Coca-Cola girl, and the public, personified as Jim.

In 1930, Coca-Cola began sponsoring a radio show that featured celebrity hosts. This show was expanded in 1934 and 1935. Complete with a sixty-five piece orchestra and a twenty-five member vocal group, "The Pause That Refreshes" was a half-hour of popular music with three Coca-Cola advertisements.

Until the advent of television in the early 1950s, the Coca-Cola Company sponsored a wide variety of radio programs. One memorable show began in November of 1941 and was called "Spotlight Bands." The show featured a series of different bands selected to entertain young Americans in the Armed Forces.

Other programs featured such radio and music stars as Percy Faith, Spike Jones, Edgar Bergen and Charlie McCarthy, and Mario Lanza. Although Coca-Cola began to focus more on television advertising in the 1950s, it had its greatest radio hit in 1970 with a song called, "I'd Like to Buy the World a Coke." The song was so successful that Coca-Cola revised it and changed the title to, "I'd Like to Teach the World to Sing." The two versions sold over one million copies with all the proceeds going to UNICEF.

Because there are people who save only old radio serials, it is possible to find and own a nice collection of Coca-Cola broadcasts.

Radios

Cola-Cola didn't use radios for advertising until the 1930s. The radios always resemble either a cooler, bottle, or can.

Cooler radio, 1949, **$400.**

Bottle radio, 1930, **$800.**

Crystal radio, 1950, **$85.**

Transistor, 7½″ × 3½″, 1963, **$75.**

Coke can radio, 1971, **$15.**

Transistor, 4½″ × 2½″, 1963, **$85.**

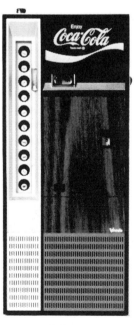

Transistor, 1972, **$65.**

Records and music

Sheet music, 13½″ × 10½″, 1905, set **$500.**

A similar set including "Old Folks at Home," "Juanita," "Lead Kindly Light," and "Nearer, My God to Thee" also worth $500 was found in a piano bench recently when an estate was settled.

Sheet music, 8″ × 10½″, 1928, **$150.**

Morton Downey record, 1940. Famous radio singer, **$25.**

Training record, 16″ dia., 1945. Used for training employees, **$25.**

Tony Bennett record, 1951, **$10.**

continued on page 105

Lillian Russell oilcloth, 25″ × 44″, 1904, **$3,000.**

Hilda Clark, tin, 20″ × 28″, 1900, **$3,500.**

Cameo mirror, 6′×4′, 1905, **$7,000.**

Leaded glass, Tiffany-style chandelier,
$22'' \times 11'' \times 7\frac{1}{2}''$, 1910, **$3,000.**

Cylindrical gum, 1902, **$500.**

Oval change tray, $4^3/_8'' \times 6^1/_8''$,
"Coca-Cola Girl," 1909, **$125.**

Oval change tray, $4^3/_8'' \times 6^1/_8''$,
1912, **$85.**

Cigar band, 1927, **$100.**

Metalcraft truck, 11″ long, 1930, **$275.**
With working headlights, **$400.**

Buddy Lee doll,
12½" tall, 1928,
$400.

Santa Claus, 1940, **$150.**

Salesman's sample cooler, 1934, **$1,500.**

Records and music,

continued

Sheet music, 1971, cover.

"It's the Real Thing," 1971, **$4.**

Sheet music, 1971, **$15.**

Sheet music, 1969, **$7.**

Record series, 1971: "The Lone Ranger," "Superman," "Sgt. Preston of The Yukon," and "Dick Tracy." These are the actual old radio shows that were part of the afternoon series. Coca-Cola advertisements appear on the backs of the albums, each **$25.**

W. C. Fields record, 1971. Part of the same afternoon series. This particular album is more valuable because of the girls photographed on the front, **$40.**

St. Nicholas and Coke

The bishop of Myra lived in the country of Lycia in Asia Minor around 300 A.D. It was this man with the gentle nature and dedication to children and mankind that the legend of St. Nicholas is based on.

In 1882, Clement Clarke Moore's poem "Twas the Night Before Christmas," promoted St. Nicholas' image as that of a pixie-like character.

The image of Santa Claus changed over the years. By 1931, the artist Haddon Sundblom had developed a realistic portrait of Santa Claus that would be used in Christmas advertisements for years to come.

Some characteristics of Haddon's Santa were white hair and a long beard, a long red coat trimmed in white fur, a leather belt with a buckle, and high boots.

Santa Claus memorabilia can make a very fascinating collection. The following slogans connected Santa and Coca-Cola on cards, billboards, magazine advertisements, blotters, etc.

"The Busiest Man in the World comes up smiling after . . . the pause that refreshes," 1930 (this was the first Coke advertisement with Santa Claus in it)

"Please Pause Here, Jimmy," 1932

"Away with a tired thirsty face. Bounce back to normal," 1933 (shows Santa taking off a tired yawning face)

"The pause that keeps you going," 1934

"It will refresh you too," 1935

"Me too. The pause that refreshes," 1936

"Give and take, say I," 1937 (shows Santa drinking a bottle of Coke and eating a piece of chicken from someone's refrigerator)

"Thanks for the pause that refreshes," 1938

"And the same to you," 1939

"Somebody knew I was coming," 1940

"Thirst asks nothing more," 1941
"Drink Coca-Cola," 1943
"Here's to G.I. Joes," 1944 (Sprite and Santa)
"They knew what I wanted," 1945
"For me," 1946
"Busy man's pause," 1947
"Hospitality," 1948
"For Santa," 1950
"Now it's my time," 1951
"Almost everyone appreciates the best," 1955
"Twas the Coke before Christmas," 1956
"Santa's pause," 1958 (shows Santa taking off his boots)

After 1960, Santa advertisements included popular slogans such as "Things go better with Coke."

Signs (Festoons)

Bottle tray, 20″ × 10⅛″, 1900, **$1,500.**

Celluloid bottle sign, 1900, **$1,500.**

Hilda Clark, tin, 20″ × 28″, 1899,
$5,000.

Hilda Clark, paper, 15″ × 20″, 1900, **$1,500.**

Lillian Nordica, cardboard, 25″ × 39″, 1904, **$900.**

Lillian Nordica, oval, 8¼″ × 10¼″, 1903, **$3,500.**

Betty, tin, 30″ × 40″, 1914, **$900.**

Elaine, tin, 20″ × 30″, 1917, **$750.**

St. Louis Fair, cardboard, 28″ × 44″,
1904, **$3,000.**

Cameo matte poster, 1904, **$1,200.**

Tin, 27″ × 19″, 1907, **$200.**

Coca-Cola in bottles, chrome 1920, **$85.**

Cherub, 1908, **$600.**
Stand-up version with easel back (rare), **$900.**

Arrow, tin, 30″ × 7¾″, 1927, **$100.**

Coca-Cola girls, cardboard, 1922, **$400.**

Bottle, tin, 3′, 1923, **$100.**

Tin sign, 13″ × 6″, 1931, **$50.**

Wooden sign, dated 1935, **$70.**

Plastic sign, 9″ diameter, c. 1940, **$30.**

Porcelain sign, dated 1950, **$65.**

Other signs not pictured include:

Cardboard die-cut, 1912,
  18″ × 21″ $450
Paper signs, 1920, 12″ × 20″
  Delicious and Refreshing . . 100
  Pause a Minute — Refresh
    Yourself 100
  That Taste Good Feeling . . . 125
  Treat Yourself Right 125
Paper signs, 1929, 10″ × 30″
  An Ice Cold with a Red
    Hot 175
  Off to a Fresh Start 175
It's Delicious, cardboard,
  9″ × 12″, 1930 75
Cut-out window displays,
  1932
  Joan Blondell 450
  Sue Carol 400
  Jean Harlow 500
  Lupe Velez 450
Paper sign, 1932, 11″ × 21½″,
  Lupe Velez 200
Wallace Beery, cardboard,
  14″ × 29″, 1934 125

Wallace Beery and Jackie
  Cooper, 1934, 4½
  foot-long window display
  piece 400
Cardboard, 14″ × 30″, 1936
  Ice Cold 75
  It Cools You 100
  Refreshing 100
Large cardboard signs,
  29″ × 50″
  50th Anniversary, 1936 . . . 250
  "For people on the go,"
    1940 50
  "He's coming home tomorrow,"
    1940s 40
  Home-Refreshment, 1940s . . 75
  The year-round answer to thirst,
    1941 100
  Refreshment Right out of the
    Bottle, 1942 75
Superstar cardboard signs,
  11″ × 14″, 1950s
  Roy Campanella, Sugar Ray
    Robinson, Monte Irvin, Bill
    Bruton, Larry Doby,
    Satchel Paige, and Lionel
    Hampton 150

Festoons

Other festoons, collectible but not shown, are:

Coca-Cola girls, 1927 . . . . . . $400
Coca-Cola girls, 1951 150
Coca-Cola girls, 1958 100
Backbar displays
  Antique cars, 1950 100

Square dance, 1950 100
State tree, 1950 100
Girls' heads, 1951 100
Festoons connected by ribbons
  Cornflower 350
  Hollyhock 400
  Morning glory 400
  Verbena 300

Smoking Paraphernalia

Match safes and holders were useful and elegant for carrying wooden matches; however, they were expensive to manufacture. Later, paper matches were produced easily and inexpensively. However, they were less durable and therefore are more difficult to find.

Matchbooks not pictured include:

Ask for a Bottle, 1908 ..... $175

Matchbook holder, 1906, **$100.**

Match safe, brass, 1908. Many people collect match safes of all types—embossed, engraved, or embroidered, **$200.**

Matchbook holder, 1907, **$100**.

Celluloid matchbook holder, 1910, **$75.**

Silver ashtray, 1930, **$15.**

Solid brass ashtray, fiftieth anniversary, 1936, **$25.**

Cigarette box, frosted glass, fiftieth anniversary, 1936, **$100.**

Four-suit ashtrays, 1940. Very popular and hard to find, **$75.**

Crinkled ashtray, 1950, **$20.**

Can lighter, 1950, **$30.**

Match holder ashtray, unique, 1940, **$200.**

Musical lighter, "Things go better with Coke," 1960, **$35.**

Miniature lighter, 1950, **$20.**

Thermometers

Many people collect thermometers exclusively. There are over one hundred different thermometers.

Other collectible thermometers not pictured include:

Wooden, 1900 . . . .$275
Wooden, 1905 275
Tin bottle, 17″, 1930 50
Tin, oval with bottle, 7″ ×
  16″, 1936 35
Tin bottle, 17″, 1950 20
Tin bottle, 17″, 1958 15

Two-bottled thermometer, 1941, **$50.**

Drink Coca-Cola, 1939, **$50.**

Toys

Other toys not pictured:

Whistle, 1940 . . . . $35	Comic book, 1951 35
Bank, 1948 15	Coke bank, 1960 7
Cap bank, 1950 10	Magic kit, 1965 35
Model plane, 1950 25	Puzzle in a can, 1968 25
Ping-Pong paddles, 1950 30	Frisbee, 1970 10
	Beanbag, 1971 20

American Flyer kite, 1930, **$300.**

Circus cutouts, 1930, **$50.**

Bingo, 1930, **$12.**

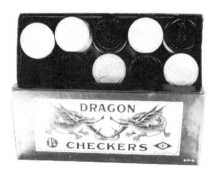

Checkers, 1930, **$30.**

Cribbage board, 1930, **$30.**

Dart board, 1935, **$45.**

Toy stove, 1938, **$500.**

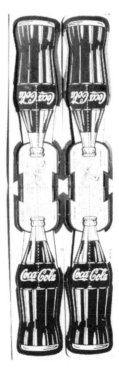

Toy train car, 1938, **$150.**

Boomerang, 1940, **$30.**

Tick-tack-toe, 1940, **$65.**

Marbles, 1950, **$25.**

Darts, 1940, **$30.**

Dominos, 1940, **$35.**

Dispenser, 1960, **$75.**   Yo-yo, 1960, **$25.**

Bang gun, 1960, **$20.**

Puzzle, 1960, **$20.**

BINGO				
12	25	41	51	63
3	30	37	54	66
7	21	Coca-Cola	56	74
1	26	35	50	69
10	17	45	47	64

Bingo, 1960, **$5.**

Trays

Standard sizes for trays are: early, dated round, 9½″ diameter; matching round change trays, 5½″ diameter; and large ovals, 12½″ × 15¼″. The rectangular trays were eventually standarized to measure 10½″ × 13¼″. Trays illustrated are standard sizes unless otherwise noted.

Victorian girl, 1898, **$4,500-5,000.**

Hilda Clark, 1899, **$2,500-2,900.**
Matching change tray, **$1,500.**

Hilda Clark, 9¾″ dia., 1900, **$2,000.**
Matching change tray, **$1,000.**

St. Louis Fair, 10¾″ dia., 1904, **$350.**
Matching large oval, 13¾″ × 16½″,
$700.
Small change tray, 4″ × 6″, **$175.**

Bottle tray, 9¾″ dia., 1900, **$3,500.**
Matching change tray, **$2,500.**

Hilda Clark, 9¾″ dia., 1903, **$1,500.**
Matching change tray, 6″ dia., **$750.**
Matching change tray 4″ dia., **$600.**
Large 15″ × 18½″ tray, **$2,500.**

Lillian Russell, 10½″ × 13″ oval, 1904, $850. There is another version of this tray that shows a bottle displayed on the table in place of the glass.

Juanita, 10¾″ × 13¼″ dia., 1905, $650.
Matching change tray, 4″ dia., $250.

Relieves Fatigue, 10½″ × 13″ oval, 1906, $750.
Large oval, $850.
Small change tray, $250.

Coca-Cola girl, 1909, $350.
Oval change tray, $175-200.
Large oval, $850.

Signed by Hamilton King, 1912, **$250.**
Matching change tray, $4^3/_8'' \times 6^1/_8''$,
$120-150.

Betty, 1914, **$175-200.**
Large oval, **$250.**
Change tray, **$90-120.**

Elaine, $8^1/_2'' \times 19''$, 1917, **$175-200.**
Change tray, **$90-120.**
This tray shape was produced in 1917
only.

Garden girl, 1920, **$250.**
Large oval, $13^3/_4'' \times 16^1/_2''$, **$500.**
Change tray, **$175.**

ummer girl, 1921, **$250-275.**

Autumn girl, 1922, **$250.**

Flapper girl, 1923, **$175.**

Smiling girl, 1924, **$200-250.**

Girl at party, 1925, **$150.**

Sports couple, 1926, **$200.**

Curb service, 1927, **$190.**

Soda fountain clerk, 1927, **$150.**

irl with bobbed hair, 1927, **$150.**

Girl in swimsuit holding glass, 1929, **$125.**
Girl in swimsuit holding bottle (more unusual), **$200.**

irl with a telephone, 1930, **00-150.**

Bathing beauty, 1930, **$125-150.**

Farm boy with dog, 1931, **$250.**

Bathing beauty, 1932, **$200.**

Francis Dee, 1933, **$125-150.**

Maureen O'Sullivan and Johnny
Weissmuller, 1934, **$300.**

Madge Evans, 1935, **$75-100.**

Hostess, 1936, **$75-100.**

Running girl, 1937, **$75-100.**

Girl in the afternoon, 1938, **$50-85.**

Sailor girl, 1940, **$60-85.**

Springboard girl, 1939, **$60-85.**

Girl ice skater, 1941, **$60-85.**

Two girls at car, 1941, **$60-85.**

Girl with wind in her hair, 1943, **$25.**

Girl with menu, 1950, **$20-45.**
French version of this tray is worth
more.

TV tray, 1956, **$25.**

Girl with the umbrella, 1957, **$100.**

Rooster tray, 1957, **$75.**

Birdhouse tray, 1957, **$75.**

Western Coca-Cola Bottling Company Vienna art plates, 1905, each **$400.** In 1905, the Vienna Art Company made a variety of plates advertising bakeries, taverns, haberdasheries, and Coca-Cola. The metal plates had very ornate frames and were packed in wooden, velvet-lined cases. Western Coca-Cola Bottling Company used the Vienna art plates for advertising instead of the conventional Coke trays. The company, in Chicago, Illinois, was a subsidiary of the Coca-Cola Company, and provided syrup and advertising items to bottlers within its territory. As Coke memorabilia, these trays are valuable simply because of the stamp on the back: "Vienna Art Plates, Pat. Feb. 21st 1905, Western Coca-Cola Bottling Co."

TV tray, picnic basket, 1958, **$35.**

Pansy garden, 1961, **$25.**
Tray may be found with either "Coke refreshes you best" or "Be really refreshed."

Lillian Russell, 1968, **$50.**

Lillian Nordica, 1969, **$35.**
Also a version in French.

1909, reproduced in 1971, **$10.**
Reproduction trays can be identified
by the date on the rim. Also,
trademark is not enclosed in the
fishtail of the C in the logo.

1912, reproduced in 1972, **$10.**

1914, reproduced in 1972, **$20.**

1917, reproduced in 1972, **$20.**

Wallets and coin purses

Other collectible wallets not shown:

Wallet, 1912 . . . . $90

Embossed wallet, 1915 60
Wallet, 1922 75
Billfold, 1928 50

Engraved coin purse, 1906, **$100.**

Embossed coin purse, 1906, **$100.**

Two-sided coin purse, 1910, **$75.**

Change purse, 1910, **$75.**

Billfold, 1912, **$80.**

Wallet, 1919, **$80.**

Wallet, 1970, **$10.**

Embossed wallet, 1928, **$55.**

Watch fobs

No one wore a wristwatch in early 1900. Instead, people wore pocket watches with watch fobs. The timepiece was attached to the fob with a piece of leather. The watch fobs were generally 1¾ " × 1¼ " × 1½ ".

Others not pictured:

Girl sitting on bench,
1900 . . . . $350

Hilda Clark, 1900 300
Oval, celluloid and metal,
1905 250
Girl in car, 1½ " × 2",
1906 200
Girl with bottle, 1906 300
Rectangle, metal Coca-Cola,
1908 100
Drink Coca-Cola, 1925 75

Silver or brass, 1908, **$75.**

Metal, girl, 1917, **$150.**

Metal, dogs, 1925, **$85.**

Source directory

Books

Coca-Cola, An Illustrated History, Pat Watters, 1978, Doubleday and Company, Garden City, NY.

Excellent look into the strategy behind the building of the Coke empire.

Coca-Cola Collectibles, Volumes I-IV, Shelly and Helen Goldstein, 1970, 1973, 1974, 1975, P.O. Box 4761, Santa Barbara, CA 93103.

Features hundreds of full-color photographs. These books are widely used and referred to in correspondence, trading, and advertising by collectors around the world.

Golson's Unique and Varied Bottles, Golson Hook, 75 Roswell Street, Alpharetta, GA 30201.

Lists the values of bottles from most local bottlers.

The Illustrated Guide to the Collectibles of Coca-Cola, Cecil Munsey, 1972, Hawthorn Books, NY.

A good accounting of Coca-Cola history. Some photographs.

The Index to Coca-Cola Collectibles, Shelly and Helen Goldstein, 1982, P.O. Box 4761, Santa Barbara, CA 93103.

An updated price guide and index, this book is designed to be used alone or with the four *Coca-Cola Collectibles* volumes. Each item is indexed alphabetically and cross-referenced by date. Includes fifty full-color photographs.

Monthly Publications

American Collector
Drawer C
Kermit, TX 79745

Provides a broad market in which one can advertise collectibles.

The Antique Trader
P.O. Box 1050
Dubuque, IA 52001

An excellent newspaper for collectors of everything.

Rarities
P.O. Box 667
Beaumont, CA 92223

A general hobby magazine.

Other publications are available from these two companies:

The Nostalgia Company
21 South Lake Drive
Hackensack, NJ 07601

This company sponsors a mail-order auction. For four dollars you receive three auction catalogs that describe Coca-Cola, Pepsi Cola, Hires, Orange Crush, and Moxie advertising collectibles.

Palmetto Warehouse
Highway 321
Norway, SC 29113

Write for catalog of novelty Coke items.

Note: There are some mail order auction houses that do not grade the condition of sale items. Always try to establish an accurate description of items you intend to buy through the mail.

Museums

Calamity Jane's Ice Cream House
and Coca-Cola Museum
Sam's Town
5111 Boulder Highway
Las Vegas, NV
(800) 634-6371

This ice cream house and museum is one of a kind. The nostalgic soda fountain is decorated with the most elite collectibles, including three glass chandeliers, a solid brass cash register, and several porcelain syrup dispensers. More than three hundred items are permanently displayed for view from 10 a.m. to 1 a.m. They also serve marvelous ice cream made from the finest ingredients.

The Cola Mill
Persimmon Hollow Antique
Village
1 block East of 71st and Garnett
Tulsa, OK 74114
(918) 582-5986

This very small 9-foot × 13-foot shop is open Saturdays and Sundays 9 a.m. to 5 p.m. Steve Ellsworth, the owner, is supplementing his display area with a 10-foot × 15-foot addition. When the shop first opened in 1981, the local Coca-Cola bottler painted an

The Cola Mill.

8-foot reproduction of a 3-foot, 1939 sign for their paddle wheel. Besides Coca-Cola, the store sells Dr. Pepper, Pepsi, Orange Crush, Grapette, and other soda-related items.

The Real Thing
11650 Riverside Drive
North Hollywood, CA
(213) 980-3444

Choose your pleasure from at least three thousand Coca-Cola items for sale.

Schmidt's Marvelous Museum
Elizabethtown, KY
(502) 737-4000

The Schmidt Museum is located in the Coca-Cola Bottling Company in Elizabethtown. After touring the museum, visitors have a chance to view modern bottling procedures. The Museum is open Monday through Friday from 9 a.m. to 4 p.m.

The Cola Mill.

Antique Stores

Betty's Country Shop
Highway A1A
Fernandina, FL 32034

Charro & Company
10700 Hammerly, Suite 102
Houston, TX 77043
(713) 464-6911
Open six days a week, sells advertising antiques of all kinds.

Country Corner Flea Market
P.O. Box 1140, 585 North Jefferson
Lebanon, MO 65536

Countryside Emporium
P.O. Box 289
Lisbon, OH 44432

County Line Antiques
Box 1439
Aldergrove, BC V0X1A0

Covered Wagon Trading Post
Route 3, Box 156
Daleville, AL 36322

Curtis & MacKnight Antiques
426 North 19th Street
Houston, TX 77008
(713) 862-8638
Open four to five days a week, sells advertising antiques.

Hob Knob Shop
Knob Lick, MO 63651

Ken and Alva Higgins
Cole's Flea Market
Pearland, TX 77581
Open weekends.

McMurray Antiques
Box 404
Windsor, NY 13865

Nickelodean
13826 Ventura Boulevard
Sherman Oaks, CA 91403
(213) 981-5325

Pearl Brown Antiques
535 Whalley Avenue
New Haven, CT 06511

Southeastern Antiques
141 North Myrtle
Jacksonville, FL 32204

Sullivans Antiques
Box 47
New Market, MD 21774

Bob Buffaloe and
the Cola Clan

Coca-Cola memorabilia collector, Bob Buffaloe, is not one who takes his hobbies lightly. This Memphis, Tennessee, man decorates his entire house with Coke artifacts. Bob's enthusiasm for Coke memorabilia started modestly with the purchase of an old Coca-Cola thermometer for one dollar. His hobby has grown into what may be called an obsession. This obsession drove Bob to start the Cola Clan in November of 1974.

The Cola Clan is a national group of Coke memorabilia collectors, numbering over two thousand five hundred and spanning eight countries. For a twelve dollar annual membership fee, the club offers nationwide communication with other collectors. There is a comprehensive monthly newsletter with free want ads. I have seen advertisements with entire collections for sale. This newsletter presents an opportunity to find rarer items.

You can write for information about the Cola Clan at: The Cola Clan, c/o A. Fisher, 2084 Continental Drive NE, Atlanta, GA 30345.

Coca-Cola bottling companies

Available in more than one hundred thirty five countries at four million retail outlets, Coca-Cola is served at a rate of one hundred seventy five million servings per day. Throughout the world, more than one thousand six hundred independent Coca-Cola bottling companies are responsible for bringing the refreshment and enjoyment of Coca-Cola to people in their local communities. A list of these bottling companies arranged by state follows. Within each state, bottling companies are listed in alphabetical order according to the cities in which they are located.

Alabama

Chambers Bottling Company
Highway 431 South
Albertville, AL 35950

Meridian Coca-Cola Bottling
104 Broad Street
Aliceville, AL 35442

Montgomery Coca-Cola Bottling
401 Cherokee Road
Alexander City, AL 35010

Coca-Cola Bottling Company
239 Church Street
Andalusia, AL 36420

Coca-Cola's Central Avenue headquarters in Los Angeles, with its famed flagship facade, has long been a Los Angeles landmark. While the interior of the building was almost completely remodeled during 1975 and 1976 to create pleasant surroundings, and accommodate future expansion, a particular point was made of preserving the best of the old in architectural details and design. This facade has now been dedicated as a historic monument—a symbol of the city's cultural and economic heritage.

Coca-Cola Bottling Company
P.O. Box 1060
Anniston, AL 36202

Coca-Cola Bottling Company
4600 East Lake Boulevard
Birmingham, AL 35217

Birmingham Coca-Cola Bottling
Highway 69, P.O. Box 219
Cullman, AL 35055

Decatur Coca-Cola Bottling
Company
1 Refreshment Place
Decatur, AL 35601

Coca-Cola Bottling Company
310 North St. Andrews Street
Dothan, AL 36303

Florence Coca-Cola Bottling
502 South Court Street
Florence, AL 35630

Montgomery Coca-Cola Bottling
Bowden Street
Frisco City, AL 36445

Alabama Coca-Cola Bottling
644 Walnut Street
Gadsden, AL 35902

Coca-Cola Bottling Company
Railroad Avenue
Gordo, AL 35466

Birmingham Coca-Cola Bottling
Old 278 Highway
Guin, AL 35563

Ripps, Irving & Sons
62 St. Louis Street
Mobile, AL 36633

Wometco Coca-Cola Bottling
   Company
Coca-Cola Road
Mobile, AL 36601

Coca-Cola Bottling Company
226 North Perry Street
Montgomery, AL 36197

Coca-Cola Bottling Company
P.O. Box 631
Opelika, AL 36801

Alabama Coca-Cola Bottling
701 West Hamric Drive
Oxford, AL 36203

Coca-Cola Bottling Company
248 East Lauderdale Street
Russellville, AL 35653

Coca-Cola Bottling Company
112 Green Street
Selma, AL 36701

Alabama Coca-Cola Bottling
3491 Talladega Highway
Sylacauga, AL 35150

Alabama Coca-Cola Bottling
1300 Ward Avenue
Talladega, AL 35160

Coca-Cola Bottling Company
Brundidge Street
Troy, AL 36081

Coca-Cola Bottling Company
2301 Eighth Street
Tuscaloosa, AL 35401

Alabama Coca-Cola Bottling
   Company
U.S. Highway 431 South
Wedowee, AL 36278

York Coca-Cola Bottling
1022 Fourth Avenue
York, AL 36925

Alaska
Odom Corporation
240 First Avenue
Anchorage, AK 99501

Alaska Beverage Company
Phillips Road
Fairbanks, AK 99701

Ketchikan Soda Works
Box 7600
Ketchikan, AK 99901

Sitka Bottling
P.O. Box 197
Sitka, AK 99835

Arizona
Coca-Cola Bottling Company
936 F Avenue
Douglas, AZ 85607

Simon, Mike E. Company
P.O. Box 1045
Douglas, AZ 85607

Wometco Coca-Cola Bottling
P.O. Box 413
Flagstaff, AZ 86001

3 G Counties Coca-Cola
383 South Hill Street
Globe, AZ 85501

Wometco Coca-Cola Bottling
   Company
P.O. Box 3155
Kingman, AZ 86401

Arizona Canning Company
50 South 43 Avenue
Phoenix, AZ 85005

Coca-Cola Bottling Company
2225 East Buckeye Road
Phoenix, AZ 85009

Phoenix Coca-Cola Bottling
P.O. Box 20008
Phoenix, AZ 85036

Saguaro Beverage Supply
1915 East Buchannan
Phoenix, AZ 85034

Coca-Cola Bottling Company
202 West Eighth Street
Safford, AZ 85546

Wometco Coca-Cola Bottling
   Company
P.O. Box 818
Show Low, AZ 85901

Coca-Cola Bottling Company
3939 North Romero Road
Tucson, AZ 85705

Wometco Coca-Cola Bottling
   Company
1941 West Second Street
Winslow, AZ 86047

Haines & Sons Distributing
   Company
439 Gila Street
Yuma, AZ 85364

Arkansas
Coca-Cola Bottling Company
South Seventh Street
Arkadelphia, AR 71923

Coca-Cola Bottling Company
100-103 East College Street
Batesville, AR 72501

Jonesboro Coca-Cola Bottling
611-615 West Ash Street
Blytheville, AR 72315

Coca-Cola Bottling Company
123 Jefferson Street SE
Camden, AR 71701

Coca-Cola Bottling Company
1102 East Hillsboro Street
El Dorado, AR 71730

Fayetteville Coca-Cola Company
Township Road
Fayetteville, AR 72701

Coca-Cola Bottling Company
3600 Phoenix Avenue
Fort Smith, AR 72906

Coca-Cola Bottling Company
322 Market Street
Hot Springs, AR 71901

Coca-Cola Bottling Company
2215 East Highland Drive
Jonesboro, AR 72401

Coca-Cola Bottling Company
6901 Murray Street
Little Rock, AR 72209

Magnolia Coca-Cola Bottling
114-12 South Madison Street
Magnolia, AR 71753

Coca-Cola Bottling Company
Mann Road and Poplar Street
Marianna, AR 72360

Coca-Cola Bottling Company
Intersection of Highways 81 and 4
Monticello, AR 71655

Coca-Cola Bottling Company
P.O. Box 1560
Nashville, AR 71852

Coca-Cola Bottling Company
205 East Second Avenue
Pine Bluff, AR 71601

Coca-Cola Bottling Company
215 West Poplar Street
Rogers, AR 72756

Coca-Cola Bottling Company
510 East Lincoln Street
Searcy, AR 72143

Canners-Eastern Arkansas
1400 Rainer Road
West Memphis, AR 72301

California
Caldwell Distributing Company
406 North Court Street
Alturas, CA 96101

Catalina Beverage Company, Inc.
18 Pebbly Beach Road
Avalon, CA 90704

Coca-Cola Bottling Company
414 Nineteenth Street
Bakersfield, CA 93301

Coca-Cola Bottling Company
26677 West Main Street
Barstow, CA 92311

Coca-Cola Bottling Company
Drawer N
Blythe, CA 92225

Home Pack Beverage
212 North Buena Vista Street
Burbank, CA 91504

Coca-Cola Bottling Company
1260 Diamond Way
Concord, CA 94520

Coca-Cola Bottling Company
1335 Albee Street
Eureka, CA 95501

Coca-Cola Bottling Company
905 R Street
Fresno, CA 93721

Pricketts Distributing
123 M Street
Fresno, CA 93721

Oliveto Distributing Company
P.O. Box 848
Jackson, CA 95642

Shoshone Coca-Cola Bottling
2048 Dunlap Lane
Lake Tahoe, CA 95731

CFS Continental
2300 East 57th Street
Los Angeles, CA 90058

Coca-Cola Bottling Company
1334 South Central Avenue
Los Angeles, CA 90021

Coca-Cola Bottling Company
1430 Melody Road
Marysville, CA 95901

Modesto Coca-Cola Bottling
1520 Princeton Avenue
Modesto, CA 95352

Coca-Cola Bottling Company
2090 Fremont
Monterey, CA 93940

Coca-Cola Bottling Company
1340 Cypress Street
Oakland, CA 94607

High Sierra Beverage Company
529 Bell Lane
Quincy, CA 95971

Coca-Cola Bottling Company
1580 Beltline Road
Redding, CA 96003

Sacramento Coca-Cola Bottling
2200 Stockton Boulevard
Sacramento, CA 95816

Coca-Cola Bottling Company
251 West Market Street
Salinas, CA 93901

Coca-Cola Bottling
499 East Mill Street
San Bernardino, CA 92408

Coca-Cola Bottling Company
1348 47th Street
San Diego, CA 92102

Coca-Cola Bottling
1500 Mission Street
San Francisco, CA 94103

Coca-Cola Bottling Company
1555 Old Bayshore Highway
San Jose, CA 95112

Coca-Cola Bottling Company
14655 Wicks Boulevard
San Leandro, CA 94577

Coca-Cola Bottling Company
6100 Soquel Avenue
Santa Cruz, CA 95062

Coca-Cola Bottling Company
Jones and McClelland Streets
Santa Maria, CA 93454

Sierra Beverage
P.O. Box 98
Soulsbyville, CA 95372

Coca-Cola Bottling Company
1100 North Wilson Way
Stockton, CA 95205

Mountain Distributing Company
2102 Main Street
Susanville, CA 96130

Sacramento Coca-Cola Bottling
650 Babcock Lane
Ukiah, CA 95482

Coca-Cola Bottling Company
1609 Sears Point Road
Vallejo, CA 94590

Coca-Cola Bottling
5335 Walker Street
Ventura, CA 93003

Coca-Cola Bottling Company
350 North Foothill Drive
Yreka, CA 96097

Colorado
Alamosa Coca-Cola Bottling
   Company
701 Twenty-Second Street
Alamosa, CO 81101

Coca-Cola Bottling Company
415 West Pikes Peak Avenue
Colorado Springs, CO 80905

Denver Coca-Cola Bottling
   Company
3825 York Street
Denver, CO 80205

Westman Commission Company
P.O. Box 17469
Denver, CO 80217

Durango Coca-Cola Bottling
   Company
Seventh and Camino Del Rio
Durango, CO 81301

Coca-Cola Bottling
1009 Ensign Street
Fort Morgan, CO 80701

Coca-Cola Bottling Company
502 Twenty-Ninth Avenue
Glenwood Springs, CO 81601

Coca-Cola Bottling Company
1226 Winters Avenue
Grand Junction, CO 81502

Greeley Coca-Cola Bottling
  Company
1200 Seventh Avenue
Greeley, CO 80631

Coca-Cola Bottling Company
7495 U.S. Highway 50
Lamar, CO 81052

Coca-Cola Bottling Company
3004 South Prairie
Pueblo, CO 81004

Coca-Cola Bottling Company
100 West Elm Avenue
Rocky Ford, CO 81067

Salida Coca-Cola Bottling
  Company
1320 D Street
Salida, CO 81201

Sterling Coca-Cola Bottling
530 South Sixth Avenue
Sterling, CO 80751

Coca-Cola Bottling
1005 Independent Road
Trinidad, CO 81082

Connecticut
Coca-Cola Bottling Company
451 Main Street
East Hartford, CT 06108

Coca-Cola Bottling of NY, Inc.
450 Scofield Avenue Exit
Fairfield, CT 06430

Coca-Cola Bottling Company
310 South Main Street
Middletown, CT 06457

Coca-Cola Bottling Company
951 Bank Street
New London, CT 06320

Coca-Cola Bottling Company
75 Progress Lane
Waterbury, CT 06705

Delaware
Dover Coca-Cola Bottling
Lincoln Street
Dover, DE 19901

Delaware Coca-Cola Bottling
Lancaster and Gray Avenues
Wilmington, DE 19805

Florida
Coca-Cola Company
141 Avenue East
Apalachicola, FL 32320

Coca-Cola Bottling Company
141 North Desoto Avenue
Arcadia, FL 33821

Coca-Cola Bottling Company
23091 Cortez Boulevard
Brooksville, FL 33512

Brevard Coca-Cola Bottling
Company
695 Clearlake Road
Cocoa, FL 32922

Coca-Cola Bottling Company
4401 Ponce De Leon Boulevard
Coral Gables, FL 33146

Associated Coca-Cola Bottling
320 Orange Avenue
Daytona Beach, FL 32015

Fort Myers Coca-Cola Bottling
2403 Cleveland Avenue
Fort Myers, FL 33902

Coca-Cola Bottling Company
3939 St. Lucie Boulevard
Fort Pierce, FL 33450

Gainesville Coca-Cola Company
929 East University
Gainesville, FL 32601

Coca-Cola Bottling Company
3350 Pembroke Road
Hollywood, FL 33021

Homestead Coca-Cola Bottling
186 Southwest First Street
Homestead, FL 33030

Coca-Cola Bottling Company
1411 Huron Street
Jacksonville, FL 32205

Coca-Cola Bottling Company
7917 Atlantic Boulevard
Jacksonville, FL 32211

Coca-Cola Bottling Company
101 Simonton Street
Key West, FL 33040

Lake City Coca-Cola Bottling
900 North Alachua Street
Lake City, FL 32055

Lakeland Coca-Cola Bottling
540 North Reynolds Road
Lakeland, FL 33802

Coca-Cola Bottling Company
110 South Highway 468
Leesburg, FL 32748

Marianna Coca-Cola Bottling
Highway 90
Marianna, FL 32446

Coca-Cola Bottling Company
301 Northwest Twenty-Ninth
Miami, FL 33127

Coca-Cola Bottling Company
2870 Northeast Twenty-Fourth
Ocala, FL 32670

Orlando Coca-Cola Bottling
Company
2900 Mercy Drive
Orlando, FL 32808

Pahokee Coca-Cola Bottling
246 East Main Street
Pahokee, FL 33476

Coca-Cola Bottling
120 South Seventh
Palatka, FL 32077

Panama City Coca-Cola, Inc.
238 West Fifth Street
Panama City, FL 32401

Hygeia Coca-Cola Bottling
   Company
7330 North Davis Highway
Pensacola, FL 32504

Perry Coca-Cola Bottling
   Company
Highway 98
Perry, FL 32347

Florida Coca-Cola Bottling
   Company
3015 Cooper Street
Punta Gorda, FL 33950

Quincy Coca-Cola Bottling
   Company
305 West Crawford Street
Quincy, FL 32351

Coca-Cola Bottling Company
One Coke Drive
St. Augustine, FL 32084

Coca-Cola Bottling Company
2950 Gandy Bridge Boulevard
St. Petersburg, FL 33702

Coca-Cola Bottling
1126 North Lime Avenue
Sarasota, FL 33578

Coca-Cola Bottling Company
Highway 27 South
Sebring, FL 33870

Tallahassee Coca-Cola Company
1320 South Monroe Street
Tallahassee, FL 32301

Tampa Coca-Cola Bottling
Thirteenth Street and York
Tampa, FL 33602

Tarpon Springs Coca-Cola
Alternate Highway 19 South
Tarpon Springs, FL 33589

Hygeia Coca-Cola Bottling
   Company
678 Highway 85 A
Valparaiso, FL 32580

Wauchula Coca-Cola Bottling
300 North Florida Avenue
Wauchula, FL 33873

Coca-Cola Bottling Company
504 East Railroad Avenue
West Palm Beach, FL 33401

Georgia
Albany Coca-Cola Bottling
925 Pine Avenue
Albany, GA 31703

Americus Coca-Cola Bottling
441 Cotton Avenue
Americus, GA 31709

Athens Coca-Cola Bottling
297 Prince Avenue
Athens, GA 30603

Atlanta Coca-Cola Bottling
Company
864 Spring Street NW
Atlanta, GA 30308

Coca-Cola Bottling Company
8250 Dunwoody Place NE
Atlanta, GA 30338

Coca-Cola Bottling Company
930 Spring Street
Atlanta, GA 30309

Augusta Coca-Cola Bottling
Company
1901 North Leg Road
Augusta, GA 30903

Coca-Cola Bottling Company
450 Lee Industrial Boulevard
Austell, GA 30001

Bainbridge Coca-Cola Bottling
317 North Clay Street
Bainbridge, GA 31717

Federal Coca-Cola Bottling
Company
U.S. Highway 341
Baxley, GA 31513

Brunswick Coca-Cola Bottling
508 Mansfield Street
Brunswick, GA 31521

Carrollton Coca-Cola
217 Alabama Street
Carrollton, GA 30117

Cartersville Coca-Cola
1 North Tennessee Street
Cartersville, GA 30120

Cedartown Coca-Cola Bottling
520 Tenth Street
Cedartown, GA 30125

Claxton Coca-Cola Bottling
Company
614 West Main Street
Claxton, GA 30417

Coca-Cola Bottling Company
4755 Edison Drive
College Park, GA 30337

Coca-Cola Bottling
6055 Coca-Cola Boulevard
Columbus, GA 31908

Cordele Coca-Cola Bottling
Company
302 Sixth Street North
Cordele, GA 31015

Cornelia Coca-Cola Bottling
560 North Main Street
Cornelia, GA 30531

Cuthbert Coca-Cola Bottling
411 East Dawson
Cuthbert, GA 31740

Dalton Coca-Cola Bottling
   Company
1000 South Thornton Avenue
Dalton, GA 30720

Coca-Cola Bottling Company
2400 Mellon Court
Decatur, GA 30032

Douglas Coca-Cola Bottling
211 East Ashley Street
Douglas, GA 31533

Dublin Coca-Cola Bottling
415 East Jackson Street
Dublin, GA 31021

Fitzgerald Coca-Cola
South Grant Street
Fitzgerald, GA 31750

Fort Valley Coca-Cola Company
North Camillie Boulevard
Fort Valley, GA 31030

Coca-Cola Bottling Company
C-15 Browns Bridge Road
Gainesville, GA 30503

Atlanta Coca-Cola Bottling
410 East Taylor Street
Griffin, GA 30223

Hartwell Coca-Cola Bottling
Race and Cade Streets
Hartwell, GA 30643

Hinesville Coca-Cola Bottling
301 South Main Street
Hinesville, GA 31313

Coca-Cola Bottling Company
670 Church Street
Jasper, GA 30143

Coca-Cola Bottling Company
302 North Main Street
LaFayette, GA 30728

Coca-Cola Bottling Company
115 Broad Street
LaGrange, GA 30240

Atlanta Coca-Cola Bottling
   Company
924 Buford Drive
Lawrenceville, GA 30246

Coca-Cola Bottling Company
440 Oak Street
Macon, GA 31213

Georgia-Alabama Coca-Cola
111 North Fifth Avenue
Manchester, GA 31816

Coca-Cola Bottling Company
1091 Industrial Park Drive
Marietta, GA 30061

Federal Coca-Cola Bottling
   Company
201-215 Third Avenue
McRae, GA 31055

Milledgeville Coca-Cola
P.O. Box 1728
Milledgeville, GA 31061

Monroe Coca-Cola Bottling
424 East Spring Street
Monroe, GA 30655

Moultrie Coca-Cola Bottling
323 First Avenue NE
Moultrie, GA 31768

Atlanta Coca-Cola Bottling
167 Greenville Street
Newnan, GA 30263

Pelham Coca-Cola Bottling
Company
307-309 McLaughlin Street
Pelham, GA 31779

Richland Coca-Cola Bottling
122 Broad Street
Richland, GA 31825

Rome Coca-Cola Bottling
Sanders Drive
Rome, GA 30161

Sandersville Coca-Cola
115 South Smith Street
Sandersville, GA 31082

Savannah Coca-Cola Bottling
102 Coleman Boulevard
Savannah, GA 31402

Statesboro Coca-Cola Bottling
401 South Main Street
Statesboro, GA 30458

Swainsboro Coca-Cola Bottling
431 North Main Street
Swainsboro, GA 30401

Sylvania Coca-Cola Bottling
905 South Main Street
Sylvania, GA 30467

Atlanta Coca-Cola Bottling
312 North Hightower Street
Thomaston, GA 30286

Thomasville Coca-Cola
Company
1017 East Jackson Street
Thomasville, GA 31792

Coca-Cola Bottling Company
820 Love Avenue
Tifton, GA 31794

Valdosta Coca-Cola Company
1409 North Ashley Street
Valdosta, GA 31601

Federal Coca-Cola Bottling
Company
408 West First Street
Vidalia, GA 30474

Atlanta Coca-Cola Bottling
98 Green Street
Warner Robbins, GA 31093

Waycross Coca-Cola Bottling
101 North Nichols Street
Waycross, GA 31501

Coca-Cola Bottling Company
1700 East Tenth Street
West Point, GA 31833

Hawaii
Coca-Cola Bottling
45 Holomua Street
Hilo, HI 96720

Coca-Cola Bottling Company
449 Mapunapuna Street
Honolulu, HI 96819

Kauai Soda Company
3140 Oihana Street
Lihue, HI 96766

Maui Soda and Ice Works
918 A Lower Main Street
Wailuku, HI 96793

Idaho
Inland Coca-Cola Bottling
5858 Franklin Road
Boise, ID 83709

Payette Coca-Cola Bottling
Route 2, Seventeenth Street
Fruitland, ID 83619

Coca-Cola Bottling Company
900 East Lincoln Road
Idaho Falls, ID 83401

Clearwater Beverages, Inc.
3010 Main Street
Lewiston, ID 83501

Coca-Cola Bottling Company
1003 North Main
Pocatello, ID 83201

Twin Falls Coca-Cola Bottling
248 Third Street South
Twin Falls, ID 83301

Illinois
Coca-Cola Bottling Company
12245 South Central
Alsip, IL 60658

Coca-Cola Bottling Company
12200 South Laramie Avenue
Alsip, IL 60658

Fayette Seltzer Company
341 Shore Drive
Burr Ridge, IL 60521

Cairo-Sikeston Coca-Cola
424-428 West Eighth Street
Cairo, IL 62914

Cairo-Sikeston Coca-Cola
413 North Oakland Avenue
Carbondale, IL 62901

Coca-Cola Bottling Company
Route 161 East
Centralia, IL 62801

Coca-Cola Bottling Company
7400 North Oak Park Avenue
Chicago, IL 60648

Mattoon Coca-Cola Bottling
1405 East Main
Danville, IL 61832

Coca-Cola Bottling Company
Highway 51 South
DuQuoin, IL 62832

Coca-Cola Bottling Company
401 East Burien
Galesburg, IL 61401

Coca-Cola Bottling Company
29 West Raymond Street
Harrisburg, IL 62946

Herrin Coca-Cola Bottling
516 North Park Avenue
Herrin, IL 62948

Coca-Cola Bottling Company
1201 West Tyler
Litchfield, IL 62056

Coca-Cola Bottling Company
219 South Johnson Street
Macomb, IL 61455

Kull Packaging Corporation
2020 Prairie Avenue
Mattoon, IL 61938

Mattoon Coca-Cola Bottling
    Company
2020 Prairie
Mattoon, IL 61938

Cripe Distributing, Inc.
705 North Kaskaskia Street
Nashville, IL 62263

Coca-Cola Bottling Company
906 West Main
Olney, IL 62450

Coca-Cola Bottling Company
825 North Main
Paris, IL 61944

Peoria Coca-Cola Bottling
    Company
2421 Southwest Adams Street
Peoria, IL 61602

Peru Coca-Cola Bottling
2325 Fourth Street
Peru, IL 61354

New Salem Coca-Cola Bottling
110 East Jefferson Street
Petersburg, IL 62675

Coca-Cola Bottling Company
614 North Twenty-Fourth Street
Quincy, IL 62301

Coca-Cola Bottling Company
10400 North Second Street
Rockford, IL 61111

Coca-Cola Bottling Company
Dunham Road, Route 64
St. Charles, IL 60174

Central States Coca-Cola
3495 Sangamon Avenue
Springfield, IL 62702

Streator Coca-Cola Bottling
1109 North Bloomington
Streator, IL 61364

Indiana
Coca-Cola Bottling Company
3200 East Thirty-Eighth Street
Anderson, IN 46013

Coca-Cola Bottling Company
718 Green Boulevard
Aurora, IN 47001

Coca-Cola Bottling Company
1625 H Street
Bedford, IN 47421

Coca-Cola Bottling Company
318 South Washington Street
Bloomington, IN 47401

Coca-Cola Bottling Company
1334 Washington Street
Columbus, IN 47201

Coca-Cola Bottling Works
927 Pennsylvania Avenue
Evansville, IN 47708

Coca-Cola Bottling Company
1631 East Pontiac Street
Fort Wayne, IN 46803

Coca-Cola Bottling Company
350-360 North Jackson
Frankfort, IN 46041

Coca-Cola Bottling Company
3000 West Twenty-Fifth Street
Indianapolis, IN 46224

Coca-Cola Bottling Company
Box 109
Jasper, IN 47546

Coca-Cola Bottling Company
North Davis Road
Kokomo, IN 46901

Coca-Cola Bottling Company
305 Rumely
La Porte, IN 46350

Coca-Cola Bottling Company
830 North Sixth Street
Lafayette, IN 47902

Coca-Cola Bottling Company
Highway 54 West
Linton, IN 47441

Coca-Cola Bottling Company
82-92 South Sixth Street
Logansport, IN 46947

Coca-Cola Bottling Company
1621 South Washington Street
Marion, IN 46952

Coca-Cola Bottling Company
1701 Pidco Drive
Plymouth, IN 46563

Coca-Cola Bottling Company
1617 North Meridian
Portland, IN 47371

Richmond Coca-Cola Bottling
110 West Main
Richmond, IN 47374

Coca-Cola Bottling
P.O. Box 201
Scottsburg, IN 47170

Coca-Cola Bottling Company
405 North Harrison
Shelbyville, IN 46176

Coca-Cola Bottling Company
1818 Mishawaka Avenue
South Bend, IN 46615

Tell City Coca-Cola Bottling
321 Ninth Street
Tell City, IN 47586

Terre Haute Coca-Cola Company
924 Lafayette Avenue
Terre Haute, IN 47808

Coca-Cola Bottling Company
117 West Main Street
Washington, IN 47501

Iowa
Atlantic Bottling
4 East Second Street
Atlantic, IA 50022

Coca-Cola Bottling Company
851 Sixty-Sixth Avenue Southwest
Cedar Rapids, IA 52406

Creston Bottling Company
Highway 34 and Park Avenue
Creston, IA 50801

Coca-Cola Bottling Company
3750 West River Drive
Davenport, IA 52802

Coca-Cola Bottling Company
706 Maiden Lane
Decorah, IA 52101

Atlantic Bottling Company
4021 Fleur Drive
Des Moines, IA 50321

Kennedy, H. T. Company
11 North Twentieth Street
Fort Dodge, IA 50501

Coca-Cola Bottling
701 North Third Avenue
Marshalltown, IA 50158

Coca-Cola Bottling Company
2000 Fifteenth Street SW
Mason City, IA 50401

Coca-Cola Bottling Company
632 Gateway Drive
Ottumwa, IA 52501

Chesterman Company
4700 South Lewis Boulevard
Sioux City, IA 51102

Coca-Cola Bottling Company
120 Washington Street
Waterloo, IA 50701

Kansas
Western Bottlers, Inc.
402 West Seventh Street
Beloit, KS 67420

Coca-Cola Bottling Company
2931 West Fifteenth Street
Emporia, KS 66801

Fort Scott Coca-Cola Bottling
2522 Richard Road
Fort Scott, KS 66701

Garden City Coca-Cola
   Company
Box 816 Industrial Park
Garden City, KS 67846

Coca-Cola Bottling Company
1209 Main Street
Goodland, KS 67735

Kummer Wholesale Beverage
600 Baker Street
Great Bend, KS 67530

Coca-Cola Bottling Company
Route 4, P.O. Box 923
Independence, KS 67301

Junction City Bottling
911 North Jefferson
Junction City, KS 66441

Coca-Cola Bottling Company
646 Connecticut
Lawrence, KS 66044

Coca-Cola Bottling Company
9000 Marshall Drive
Lenexa, KS 66215

Mid-America Container
   Company
10001 Industrial Boulevard
Lenexa, KS 66215

Western Bottlers, Inc.
301 North Sixth Street
Marysville, KS 66508

Salina Coca-Cola Bottling
   Company
615 West Bishop Street
Salina, KS 67401

Topeka Coca-Cola Bottling
1717-1735 Kansas Avenue
Topeka, KS 66601

Coca-Cola Bottling Company
North Cathedral
Victoria, KS 67671

Wichita Coca-Cola Bottling
   Company
3001 East Harry
Wichita, KS 67201

Coca-Cola Bottling Company
1215 Main Street
Winfield, KS 67156

Kentucky
Western Kentucky Coca-Cola
313 Commerce Street
Bowling Green, KY 41202

Coca-Cola Bottling Company
Hodgenville Road
Campbellsville, KY 42718

Coca-Cola Bottling Company
1201 North Dixie Highway
Elizabethtown, KY 42701

Glasgow Coca-Cola Bottling
   Company
31 East Bypass
Glasgow, KY 42141

Coca-Cola Bottling Company
2303-2325 Richard Street
Hopkinsville, KY 42240

Coca-Cola Bottling Company
Leestown and Greendale Roads
Lexington, KY 40582

Louisa Coca-Cola Bottling
416 North Clay Street
Louisa, KY 41230

Coca-Cola Bottling Company
1661 West Hill Street
Louisville, KY 40210

Mid-America Canning Corporation
Tuckers School House Road
Madisonville, KY 42431

Middlesboro Coca-Cola Company
1324 Cumberland Avenue
Middlesboro, KY 40965

Owensboro Coca-Cola Bottling
4801 Frederica Street
Owensboro, KY 42301

Paducah Coca-Cola Bottling
  Company
3141 Broadway
Paducah, KY 42001

Coca-Cola Bottling Company
Cline and Steele Streets
Pikeville, KY 41501

Russellville Coca-Cola Company
141 South Winter Street
Russellville, KY 42276

Coca-Cola Bottling Company
Highway 53
Shelbyville, KY 40065

Coca-Cola Bottling Company
Long Avenue
Whitesburg, KY 41858

Louisiana

Alexandria Coca-Cola Bottling
7400 Highway 28 West
Alexandria, LA 71301

Baton Rouge Coca-Cola Company
P.O. Box 3868
Baton Rouge, LA 70821

Bogalusa Coca-Cola Bottling
213 Shenandoah Street
Bogalusa, LA 70427

Bunkie Coca-Cola Bottling
  Company
608 Southwest Main Street
Bunkie, LA 71322

Refreshment Enterprises
1101 Anson Street
Gretna, LA 70053

Coca-Cola Bottling
506 Roberts
Jennings, LA 70546

Coca-Cola Bottling Company
1314 Eraste Landry Road
Lafayette, LA 70502

DeRidder Coca-Cola Bottling
201 East Murphy
Leesville, LA 71446

oca-Cola Bottling Company
12 Pine Street
linden, LA 71055

)uachita Coca-Cola Bottling
20 at 165 Bypass
1onroe, LA 71201

Iatchitoches Coca-Cola Company
00 Parkway Drive
Iatchitoches, LA 71457

vangeline Coca-Cola Bottling
Vest Admiral Doyle Drive
Iew Iberia, LA 70560

ouisiana Coca-Cola Bottling
050 South Jefferson Davis
Iew Orleans, LA 70125

)pelousas Coca-Cola Bottling
36 East Vine Street
)pelousas, LA 70570

tuston Coca-Cola Bottling
01-103 South Bonner
tuston, LA 71270

oca-Cola Bottling Company
05 Stoner
hreveport, LA 71163

)uachita Coca-Cola Bottling
01 East Green Street
allulah, LA 71282

ouisiana Coca-Cola Bottling
300 Lynn Avenue
hibodaux, LA 70302

Maine
Coca-Cola Bottling Company
96 Thirteenth Street
Bangor, ME 04401

Coca-Cola Bottling Company
Lower Main Street, Route 2
Farmington, ME 04938

Coca-Cola Bottling Company
1750 Lisbon Street
Lewiston, ME 04240

Coca-Cola Bottling Company
Industrial Park
Machias, ME 04654

Coca-Cola Bottling Company
Building 403, Skyway Industrial
  Park
Presque Isle, ME 04769

Coca-Cola Bottling Company
650 Main Street
South Portland, ME 04106

Maryland
Coca-Cola Bottling Company
1750 West Street
Annapolis, MD 21401

Mid-Atlantic Coca-Cola Company
2012 Hammonds Ferry Road
Baltimore, MD 21227

Mid-Atlantic Coca-Cola Company
701 North Kresson Street
Baltimore, MD 21205

Coca-Cola Bottling Company
211 Washington Street
Cambridge, MD 21613

Cooler Repair and Delivery
51 Ritchie Road
Capitol Heights, MD 20027

Mid-Atlantic Coca-Cola Company
51 Ritchie Road
Capitol Heights, MD 20027

Cumberland Coca-Cola
312 Greene Street
Cumberland, MD 21502

Coca-Cola Bottling
103 Bay Street
Easton, MD 21601

Mid-Atlantic Coca-Cola
1705 North Market Street
Frederick, MD 21701

Coca-Cola U.S.A.
7310 Ritchie Highway, Suite 210
Glen Burnie, MD 21061

Hagerstown Coca-Cola Bottling
100 Charles Street
Hagerstown, MD 21740

Coca-Cola Bottling Company
315 Juniata Street
Havre de Grace, MD 21078

Mid-Atlantic Coca-Cola Company
Charles Street
La Plata, MD 20646

Oakland Coca-Cola Bottling
Company
23 South Third Street
Oakland, MD 21550

Salisbury Coca-Cola Bottling
410 Railroad Avenue
Salisbury, MD 21801

Mid-Atlantic Coca-Cola Company
1710 Elton Road
Silver Springs, MD 20903

Westminster Coca-Cola Company
525 Old Westminster Pike
Westminster, MD 21157

Massachusetts
Coca-Cola Bottling Company
825 Granite Street
Braintree, MA 02184

Coca-Cola Bottling Company
1244 Davol Street
Fall River, MA 02722

Coca-Cola Bottling Company
160 Industrial Avenue E
Lowell, MA 01851

Marty's Soda Mix Company
77 Winsor Street
Ludlow, MA 01056

Coca-Cola Bottling Company
654 Chestnut Street
Lynn, MA 01904

Coca-Cola Bottling Company
9 B Street
Needham Heights, MA 02194

Coca-Cola Bottling Company
366 King Street
Northampton, MA 01060

Coca-Cola Bottling
45 Industrial Drive
Northampton, MA 01060

Coca-Cola Bottling Company
15 Commercial Street
Pittsfield, MA 01201

Coca-Cola Bottling Company
Junction of Routes 6 and 6A
Sagamore, MA 02561

Coca-Cola Bottling
33 Plainfield Street
Springfield, MA 01104

Coca-Cola Bottling Company
State Road
Vineyard Haven, MA 02568

Michigan
Coca-Cola Bottling Company
171 North Industrial Highway
Alpena, MI 49707

Ann Arbor Coca-Cola Bottling
1935 South Industrial
Ann Arbor, MI 48104

Coca-Cola Bottling Company
2500 Broadway
Bay City, MI 48706

Coca-Cola Bottling Company
U.S. 131 South
Cadillac, MI 49601

Coca-Cola Bottling Company
400 Race Street
Coldwater, MI 49036

Coca-Cola Bottling Company
5981 West Warren Avenue
Detroit, MI 48210

Bink's Coca-Cola Bottling
Company
3001 New Danforth Road
Escanaba, MI 48929

Coca-Cola Bottling Company
2515 Lapeer Road
Flint, MI 48503

Coca-Cola Bottling Company
3741 Patterson Avenue
Grand Rapids, MI 49508

Hancock Bottling, Inc.
1800 Birch Street
Hancock, MI 49930

Coca-Cola Bottling Company
Industrial Park Road
Iron Mountain, MI 49801

Coca-Cola Bottling
1610 Northwest Avenue
Jackson, MI 49202

Coca-Cola Bottling Company
216 Peekstock Road
Kalamazoo, MI 49003

Coca-Cola Bottling Company
3300 South Creyts Street
Lansing, MI 48917

H. W. Elson Bottling Company
950 West Washington Street
Marquette, MI 49855

Coca-Cola Bottling Company
808 South Adams Street
Mt. Pleasant, MI 48858

Coca-Cola Bottling Company
1770 East Keating
Muskegon, MI 49442

Coca-Cola Bottling Company
Harbor Springs Road
Petoskey, MI 49770

Coca-Cola Bottling Company
1130 Wide Track Drive
Pontiac, MI 48058

Great Lakes Coca-Cola Company
200 Hawthorne Avenue
St. Joseph, MI 49085

Griffin and Templeton
916 Ashmun Street
Sault Ste Marie, MI 49783

Coca-Cola Bottling Company
1031 Hastings
Traverse City, MI 49684

Coca-Cola Bottling Company
221 North Thomas
West Branch, MI 48661

Minnesota

Coca-Cola Bottling Company
106 Twelfth Avenue West
Alexandria, MN 56308

Austin Coca-Cola Bottling
1600 Northwest First Avenue
Austin, MN 55912

Coca-Cola Bottling Company
116 Third Street
Bemidji, MN 56601

Viking Coca-Cola Bottling
Company
100 Washington
Brainerd, MN 56401

Hunter's Distributing Company
Crane Lake, MN 55725

Crookston Coca-Cola Bottling
609 Marin Avenue
Crookston, MN 65716

Coca-Cola Bottling Company
30 South Central Avenue
Duluth, MN 55807

Northside Beverages
1040 East Harvey Street
Ely, MN 55731

Coca-Cola Bottling Company
832 Industrial Park Boulevard
Fergus Falls, MN 56537

North Shore Jobbing Service
East Highway 61
Grand Marais, MN 55604

Coca-Cola Bottling Company
East Highway 2
Grand Rapids, MN 55744

Coca-Cola Bottling Company
Highway 15 South
Hutchinson, MN 55350

Coca-Cola Bottling Company
300 Industrial Avenue
International Falls, MN 56649

Coca-Cola Bottling Company
201 North Front
Mankato, MN 56001

Coca-Cola Bottling
107 East Main Street
Marshall, MN 56258

Coca-Cola Bottling Company
00 Center Avenue Southeast
Minneapolis, MN 55414

Coca-Cola Bottling Company
900 First Avenue North
Moorhead, MN 56560

Coca-Cola Bottling Company
0 Sixth Street
Pine City, MN 55063

Coca-Cola Bottling Company
316 Bluff
Red Wing, MN 55066

Coca-Cola Bottling Company
1803 Fourteenth Street NW
Rochester, MN 55901

Viking Coca-Cola Bottling
4610 Rusan Street
St. Cloud, MN 56301

Coca-Cola Bottling Company
2750 Eagandale Boulevard
St. Paul, MN 55121

Coca-Cola Bottling Company
832 Seventeenth Street N
Virginia, MN 55792

Coca-Cola Bottling Company
Highway 12 West
Willmar, MN 56201

Coca-Cola Bottling Company
102 Franklin Street
Winona, MN 55987

Mississippi
Aberdeen Coca-Cola Bottling
101 Washington
Aberdeen, MS 39730

Brookhaven Coca-Cola
   Company
P.O. Box 600, Highway 51 South
Brookhaven, MS 39601

Coca-Cola Bottling Company
320 Anderson Boulevard
Clarksdale, MS 38614

Coca-Cola Bottling Works
601 West Washington Street
Corinth, MS 38834

Coca-Cola Bottling Company
162 North Street
Greenville, MS 38701

Coca-Cola Bottling Company
1000 West Park Avenue
Greenwood, MS 38930

Coast Coca-Cola Bottling
3701 Twenty-Fifth Avenue
Gulfport, MS 39501

Coca-Cola Bottling Company
Highway 49 South Bypass
Hattiesburg, MS 39401

Coca-Cola Bottling
110 Chulahoma
Holly Springs, MS 38635

Coca-Cola Bottling
206 East Washington
Houston, MS 38851

Jackson Coca-Cola Bottling
Company
1421 Highway 80 West
Jackson, MS 39205

Laurel Coca-Cola Bottling
Company
902 Ellisville Boulevard
Laurel, MS 39440

Northeast Mississippi Coca-Cola
117 North Columbus Street
Louisville, MS 39339

McComb Coca-Cola Bottling
Company
Highway 24 West
McComb, MS 39648

Meridian Coca-Cola Bottling
Company
2016 Highway 45 North
Meridian, MS 39301

Natchez Coca-Cola Bottling
Company
191 Deveraux Drive
Natchez, MS 39120

New Albany Coca-Cola Bottling
Denmill Road
New Albany, MS 38652

Newton Coca-Cola Bottling
Company
Highway 80 West
Newton, MS 39345

Coca-Cola Bottling Company
7900 Highway 57
Ocean Springs, MS 39564

Philadelphia Coca-Cola Company
431 North Center Street
Philadelphia, MS 39350

Coca-Cola Bottling
P.O. Box 156
Sardis, MS 38666

Northeast Mississippi Coca-Cola
P.O. Box 966
Starkville, MS 39759

Tupelo Coca-Cola Bottling
    Company
424 South Gloster
Tupelo, MS 38801

Coca-Cola Bottling Company
2133 Washington Street
Vicksburg, MS 39180

Yazoo Coca-Cola Bottling
305 Lintonia Avenue
Yazoo City, MS 39194

Missouri
Coca-Cola Bottling Company
118 East Church
Aurora, MO 65605

Bolivar Coca-Cola Bottling
    Company
912 West Broadway
Bolivar, MO 65613

Coca-Cola Bottling Company
905 North Orange Street
Butler, MO 64730

Coca-Cola Bottling Company
915 East Green Street
Clinton, MO 64735

Coca-Cola Bottling Company
1601 Business Loop 63 South
Columbia, MO 65201

Coca-Cola Bottling Company
605 Buckley Street
Flat River, MO 63601

Coca-Cola Bottling Company
124 Barton Street
Jackson, MO 63755

Jefferson City Coca-Cola
604 Jefferson
Jefferson City, MO 65101

Wichita Coca-Cola Bottling
    Company
1301 Virginia Avenue, Box 1179
Joplin, MO 64801

Bootheel Beverage
530 South Highway 412 Bypass
Kennett, MO 63857

Lebanon Coca-Cola Bottling
    Company
503 West Elm
Lebanon, MO 65536

Coca-Cola Bottling Company
114 West Oak
Macon, MO 63552

Coca-Cola Bottling Company
19 Worthington Drive
Maryland Heights, MO 63043

St. Louis — Ca 270 + Page ?

Jefferson City Coca-Cola
1116 Elmwood Street
Mexico, MO 65265

Coca-Cola Bottling Company
421-427 Pine Street
Poplar Bluff, MO 63901

Ozarks Coca-Cola Bottling
High Point Industrial Park
Rolla, MO 65401

Mid-America Coca-Cola
Company
813 West Sixteenth Street
Sedalia, MO 65301

Coca-Cola Bottling Company
202 West Front Street
Sikeston, MO 63801

Springfield Coca-Cola
1777 North Packer Road
Springfield, MO 65803

Trenton Coca-Cola Bottling
Company
211 West Twelfth
Trenton, MO 64683

West Plains Coca-Cola
218 West Broadway
West Plains, MO 65775

Montana
Wy-Mont Beverages
4151 First Avenue South
Billings, MT 59101

Mountain Country Distributors
1715 North Route
Bozeman, MT 59715

Coca-Cola Bottling Company
520 Cobban
Butte, MT 59701

Coca-Cola Bottling
109 Second Street South
Glasgow, MT 59230

Glendive Coca-Cola Bottling
220 South Douglas
Glendive, MT 59330

Great Falls Coca-Cola Company
933 Thirty-Eighth Street North
Great Falls, MT 59401

Coca-Cola Bottling Company
1698 A Street
Helena, MT 59604

Coca-Cola Bottling Company
451 North Main
Kalispell, MT 59901

Coca-Cola Bottling
204 First Avenue North
Lewiston, MT 49457

Wy-Mont Beverages
Palmer Street
Miles City, MT 59301

Coca-Cola Bottling Company
2010 South Third Street West
Missoula, MT 59801

Nebraska

National Drink, Inc.
234 Beach Street
Chadron, NE 69337

Lincoln Coca-Cola Bottling
701 East Dodge Street
Fremont, NE 68025

Grand Island Bottling Company
1617 South Holland Drive
Grand Island, NE 68801

Coca-Cola Bottling Company
1501 South Burlington
Hastings, NE 68901

Keenan's Beverage, Inc.
119 West Railroad Avenue
Kearney, NE 68847

Lincoln Coca-Cola Bottling
    Company
603 South Twenty-Fifth Street
Lincoln, NE 68510

Dewiss Beverages
100 North Main
Long Pine, NE 69217

Nebraska City Coca-Cola
213 Central Avenue
Nebraska City, NE 68410

Coca-Cola Bottling
P.O. Box 1143
Norfolk, NE 68701

Coca-Cola Bottling Company
2008 East Phillip Avenue
North Platte, NE 69101

Coca-Cola Bottling Company
3200 North Thirtieth Street
Omaha, NE 68111

National Drinks, Inc.
2022 East Seventeenth Street
Scottsbluff, NE 69361

Lincoln Coca-Cola Bottling
    Company
204-206 National Avenue
Superior, NE 68978

Nevada

Blach Distributing Company
131 Main Street
Elko, NV 89801

Rocky Mountain Company
1701 Avenue F
Ely, NV 89301

Shoshone Coca-Cola Bottling
25 West B Street
Fallon, NV 89406

Coca-Cola Bottling Company
424 North Main Street
Las Vegas, NV 89101

Shoshone Coca-Cola Bottling
2300 Vassar
Reno, NV 89510

New Hampshire

Coca-Cola Bottling Company
Gorham Road
Berlin, NH 03570

Coca-Cola Bottling Company
285 Main Street
Claremont, NH 03743

Coca-Cola Bottling Company
682 Main Street
Keene, NH 03431

Coca-Cola Bottling Company
128 Messer Street
Laconia, NH 03246

Salem Coca-Cola Bottling
Company
99 Eddy Road
Manchester, NH 03102

Salem Coca-Cola Bottling
Company
Wentworth Avenue
Plaistow, NH 03865

Salem Coca-Cola Bottling
Company
23 South Broadway
Salem, NH 03079

Coca-Cola Bottling Company
145 Green Street
Sommersworth, NH 03878

New Jersey
Coca-Cola Bottling Company
2 Harmon Drive
Blackwood, NJ 08012

Coca-Cola Bottling Company
411 Hackensack Avenue
Hackensack, NJ 07601

Coca-Cola Bottling Company
515 South Shore Road
Marmora, NJ 08223

Coca-Cola Bottling Company
1250 Glen Avenue
Moorestown, NJ 08057

Coca-Cola Bottling Company
911 Route 35
Neptune, NJ 07753

Coca-Cola Bottling Company
216 First Avenue
Newark, NJ 07107

Coca-Cola Bottling Company
1500 Livingston Avenue
North Brunswick, NJ 08902

Coca-Cola Bottling
263 McLean Boulevard
Paterson, NJ 07504

Beverages Unlimited
366 St. Georges Avenue
Rahway, NJ 07065

New Mexico
Coca-Cola Bottling Company
P.O. Box 85426
Albuquerque, NM 87125

Pecos Valley Coca-Cola
Company
602 South Canal Street
Carlsbad, NM 88220

Clovis Coca-Cola
800 West Seventh
Clovis, NM 88101

Deming Coca-Cola Bottling
  Company
401 Atlantic
Deming, NM 88031

Coca-Cola Bottling Company
05 East Maple
Farmington, NM 87401

Coca-Cola Bottling Company
2522 East Sixty-Sixth Avenue
Gallup, NM 87301

Pecos Valley Coca-Cola Company
1203 East Broadway
Hobbs, NM 88240

Las Cruces Coca-Cola Bottling
2100 South Valley Drive
Las Cruces, NM 88004

Southwest Canners, Inc.
2301 West Eighteenth Street
Portales, NM 88130

Coca-Cola Bottling Company
560 West San Mateo Road
Santa Fe, NM 87501

Coca-Cola Bottling Company
109 Sixth Street Southeast
Socorro, NM 87801

Coca-Cola Bottling Company
823 East Main Street
Tucumcari, NM 88401

New York
Albany Coca-Cola Bottling
  Company
38 Warehouse Row
Albany, NY 12205

Saratoga Distributing Company
3605 Sheridan Drive
Amherst, NY 14226

Rochester Coca-Cola Bottling
610 East Main Street
Batavia, NY 14020

Binghamton Coca-Cola Bottling
7 Walter Avenue
Binghamton, NY 13901

Coca-Cola Bottling Company
977 East 149th Street
Bronx, NY 10455

Coca-Cola Bottling Company
1900 Linden Boulevard
Brooklyn, NY 11207

Coca-Cola Bottling Company
570 North Main Street
Canandaigua, NY 14424

Coca-Cola Bottling Company
P.O Box 36
Dansville, NY 14437

Coca-Cola Bottling Company
899 Fairview Park Drive
Elmsford, NY 10523

Coca-Cola Bottling
74-12 Eighty-Eighth Street
Glendale, NY 11385

Associated Coca-Cola Bottling
278 South Main Street
Gloversville, NY 12078

Coca-Cola Bottling Company
1765 Express Drive North
Hauppauge, NY 11787

Elmira Coca-Cola Bottling
Company
Latta Brook Park
Horseheads, NY 14845

Coca-Cola Bottling Company
Cantiague/Brush Hollow Road
Jericho, NY 11753

Heim Beverage
Averyville Road
Lake Placid, NY 12946

Coca-Cola Bottling Company
59 Borden Avenue
Maspeth, NY 11378

Canada Dry Bottling Company
28 Liberty Avenue
Massena, NY 13662

Coca-Cola Bottling Company
R.D. 2, P.O Box 38N
Monticello, NY 12701

Coca-Cola Bottling Company
145 Huguenot
New Rochelle, NY 10801

Coca-Cola Bottling Company
10 Hempstead Road
New Windsor, NY 12550

Oneonta Coca-Cola Bottling
Company
Brown Street
Oneonta, NY 13820

Olympic Coca-Cola Bottling
Company
P.O. Box 690
Plattsburgh, NY 12901

Rochester Coca-Cola Bottling
123 Upper Falls Boulevard
Rochester, NY 14605

Finger Lakes Coca-Cola Company
Routes 5 and 20
Seneca Falls, NY 13148

Associated Coca-Cola Bottling
95 Main Street
South Glen Falls, NY 12801

Coca-Cola Bottling Company
2252 Forest Avenue
Staten Island, NY 10303

Associated Coca-Cola Bottling
Farrell Road
Syracuse, NY 13209

Coca-Cola Bottling Company
200 Milens Road
Tonawanda, NY 14150

Tupper Lake Coca-Cola Company
5 High Street
Tupper Lake, NY 12986

Watertown Coca-Cola Bottling
1304 Washington Street
Watertown, NY 13601

Coca-Cola Bottling Company
Riverhead Road
Westhampton Beach, NY 11978

North Carolina

Aberdeen Coca-Cola Bottling
203 West South Street
Aberdeen, NC 28315

Albemarle Coca-Cola Bottling
1610 East Main Street
Albemarle, NC 28001

Coca-Cola Bottling Company
1623 North Fayetteville Street
Ashboro, NC 27203

Coca-Cola Bottling Company
345 Biltmore Avenue
Asheville, NC 28802

Biscoe Coca-Cola Bottling
  Company
South Main Street
Biscoe, NC 27209

Coca-Cola Bottling Company
105 Bypass, Box 1099
Boone, NC 28607

Coca-Cola Bottling Company
2000 Fifteenth Street
Bryson City, NC 28713

Burlington Coca-Cola Bottling
825 South Main Street
Burlington, NC 27215

Coca-Cola Bottling Company
829 South Summit Avenue
Charlotte, NC 28231

Consolidated Coca-Cola
1401 West Moorhead Street
Charlotte, NC 28266

Dunn Coca-Cola Bottling
  Company
100 West Divine Street
Dunn, NC 28334

Durham Coca-Cola Bottling
  Company
3214 Hillsborough Road
Durham, NC 27705

Mid-Atlantic Coca-Cola Company
521 West Broad Street
Elizabeth City, NC 27909

Coca-Cola Company
1225 Ramsey Street
Fayetteville, NC 28301

Coca-Cola Bottling Company
752 East Main Street
Forest City, NC 28043

Coca-Cola Bottling Company
620 West Franklin Avenue
Gastonia, NC 28052

Goldsboro Coca-Cola Bottling
701 South George Street
Goldsboro, NC 27530

Coca-Cola Bottling Company
2411 High Point Road
Greensboro, NC 27420

Coca-Cola Bottling Company
630 Pitt Street
Greenville, NC 27834

Hamlet Coca-Cola Bottling
  Company
Highway 74 East
Hamlet, NC 28345

Coca-Cola Bottling Company
Highway 1A South
Henderson, NC 27536

Coca-Cola Bottling Company
824 Locust Street
Hendersonville, NC 28739

Coca-Cola Bottling Company
820 First Avenue NW
Hickory, NC 28601

Kelford Coca-Cola Bottling
Front Street
Kelford, NC 27847

East Carolina Coca-Cola
P.O. Box 337
Kinston, NC 28501

Lincolnton Coca-Cola Bottling
230 East Water Street
Lincolnton, NC 28092

Lumberton Coca-Cola Bottling
500 East First Street
Lumberton, NC 28358

Coca-Cola Bottling Company
1500 East Union Street
Morganton, NC 28655

Mount Airy Coca-Cola Bottling
Highway 89, Box 1544
Mount Airy, NC 27030

New Bern Coca-Cola Bottling
Highway 17 South
New Bern, NC 28560

North Wilkesboro Coca-Cola
  Company
Highway 268 East
North Wilkesboro, NC 28659

Plymouth Coca-Cola Bottling
111-113 East Water Street
Plymouth, NC 27962

Capital Coca-Cola Bottling
  Company
2200 South Wilmington Street
Raleigh, NC 27611

Reidsville Coca-Cola Bottling
697 South Scales
Reidsville, NC 27320

Coca-Cola Bottling Company
442 South Church Street
Rocky Mount, NC 27801

Roxboro Coca-Cola Bottling
  Company
230 Morgan Street
Roxboro, NC 27573

Consolidated Coca-Cola Company
1828 North Main Street
Salisbury, NC 28144

Coca-Cola Bottling Company
605 Hawkins
Sanford, NC 27330

Coca-Cola Bottling Company
25 East Marion Street
Shelby, NC 28150

Coca-Cola Bottling Company
817 Greenwood Road
Spruce Pine, NC 28777

Statesville Coca-Cola Company
2027 West Front Street
Statesville, NC 28677

Tarboro Coca-Cola Bottling
  Company
1406 North Main Street
Tarboro, NC 27886

Thomasville Coca-Cola
  Company
814 Lexington Avenue
Thomasville, NC 27360

Coca-Cola Bottling
905 West Fifth Street Exit
Washington, NC 27889

Whiteville Coca-Cola Company
218 Lewis Street
Whiteville, NC 28472

Wilmington Coca-Cola Bottling
921 Princess Street
Wilmington, NC 28401

Coca-Cola Bottling Company
2612 Wilco Boulevard
Wilson, NC 27893

Coca-Cola Bottling Company
730 South Marshall Street
Winston-Salem, NC 27108

North Dakota
Coca-Cola Bottling Company
3301 East Rosser Avenue
Bismarck, ND 58501

Coca-Cola Bottling Company
Highway 20 South
Devils Lake, ND 58301

Coca-Cola Bottling Company
226 West Villard
Dickinson, ND 58601

Johnston's, Inc.
Box 1006, Johnstons Avenue
Dickinson, ND 58601

Coca-Cola Bottling Company
724 North Forty-Seventh Street
Grand Forks, ND 58201

Coca-Cola Bottling Company
1016 Tenth Street SE
Jamestown, ND 58401

Coca-Cola Bottling Company
405 Ninth Street SE
Minot, ND 58701

Heinie-Richels Beverages
505 Sixth Street South
Wahpeton, ND 58075

Coca-Cola Bottling Company
223 East First Street
Williston, ND 58801

Ohio

Coca-Cola Bottling Company
111 Cascade Plaza
Akron, OH 44306

Coca-Cola Bottling Company
1560 Triplet Boulevard
Akron, OH 44309

Coca-Cola Bottling Company
4922 Navarre Road
Canton, OH 44706

Coca-Cola Bottling Company
1507 Dana Avenue
Cincinnati, OH 45207

Scioto Coca-Cola Bottling
450 East Town
Circleville, OH 43113

Cleveland Coca-Cola Bottling
3705 Carnegie Avenue
Cleveland, OH 44115

Coca-Cola Bottling Company
786 Twin Rivers Drive
Columbus, OH 43215

Coca-Cola Bottling Company
4500 Groves Road
Columbus, OH 43227

Mid-Ohio Coca-Cola Company
500 South Second Street
Coshocton, OH 43812

Dayton Coca-Cola Bottling
901 South Ludlow Street
Dayton, OH 45402

Elyria Coca-Cola Bottling
Company
1410 Lake Avenue
Elyria, OH 44035

Mid-Ohio Coca-Cola
122 Clinton Court
Findlay, OH 45840

Lima Coca-Cola Bottling
201 North Shore Drive
Lima, OH 45802

Mansfield Coca-Cola Bottling
205 North Diamond Street
Mansfield, OH 44902

Marion Coca-Cola Bottling
Company
309 North Main Street
Marion, OH 43302

Painsville Coca-Cola Bottling
8755 Munson Road
Mentor, OH 44060

Middletown Coca-Cola Bottling
1501 South University Boulevard
Middletown, OH 45042

Mid-Ohio Coca-Cola Company
250 East Main Street
Newark, OH 43055

Coca-Cola Bottling
3001 Scioto Trail
Portsmouth, OH 45662

Coca-Cola Bottling Company
423 West North Street
Springfield, OH 45504

Cameron Coca-Cola Bottling
Company
813 Stoney Hollow Boulevard
Steubenville, OH 43952

Coca-Cola Bottling Company
3970 Catawba Street
Toledo, OH 43612

Great Lakes Canning, Inc.
1882 East Highland Road
Twinsburg, OH 44087

Coca-Cola Bottling Company
531 East Indianola Avenue
Youngstown, OH 44502

Coca-Cola Bottling Company
Seventh and Harvey Streets
Zanesville, OH 43701

Mid-Atlantic Canners
1805 Kemper Court
Zanesville, OH 43701

Oklahoma
Ada Coca-Cola Bottling Company
1205 Cradduck Road
Ada, OK 74820

Coca-Cola Bottling Company
601 Todd Lane
Altus, OK 73521

Alva Coca-Cola Bottling Company
114 Flynn
Alva, OK 73717

Oklahoma Beverage Company
340 NE Washington Boulevard
Bartlesville, OK 74003

Coca-Cola Bottling Company
Methin Industrial Park
Chickasha, OK 73018

Coca-Cola Bottling Company
2310 Corbin Lane
Clinton, OK 73601

Duncan Coca-Cola Bottling
Company
1301 South Highway 81
Duncan, OK 73533

Coca-Cola Bottling Company
508 South Grand
Enid, OK 73701

Coca-Cola Bottling Company
314 West Oklahoma
Guthrie, OK 73044

Idabel Coca-Cola Bottling
Company
500 South Central Avenue
Idabel, OK 74745

Lawton Coca-Cola Bottling
Company
511 North Second
Lawton, OK 73502

McAlester Coca-Cola
218 South Second
McAlester, OK 74501

Love Bottling Company
2000 Peake Boulevard
Muskogee, OK 74401

Great Plains Coca-Cola
600 North May Avenue
Oklahoma City, OK 73147

Oklahoma Beverage Company
106 North Oklahoma
Okmulgee, OK 74447

Oklahoma Beverage Company
2501 North Ash Avenue
Ponca City, OK 74601

Love Bottling
210 North Adair Street
Pryor, OK 74361

Shawnee Bottling
Kennedy and Kickapoo
Shawnee, OK 74801

Coca-Cola Bottling Company
State Hospital Road
Vinita, OK 74301

Woodward Coca-Cola Bottling
Ninth and Sante Fe
Woodward, OK 73801

Oregon

Coca-Cola USA Company
7741 Southwest Cirrus Road
Beaverton, OR 97005

Coca-Cola Bottling Company
1212 North East Street
Bend, OR 97701

Coca-Cola Bottling Company
1565 Franklin Boulevard
Eugene, OR 97403

Gardner Enterprises
195 Northeast Second Street
John Day, OR 97845

Coca-Cola Bottling Company
105 North Spring Street
Klamath Falls, OR 97601

Coca-Cola Bottling Company
1114 Jefferson Street
La Grande, OR 97850

Coca-Cola Bottling Company
3074 Crater Lake Avenue
Medford, OR 97501

Coca-Cola Bottling Company
860 Florida
North Bend, OR 97459

Coca-Cola Bottling Company
410 Southeast Fourth
Pendleton, OR 97801

Pacific Coca-Cola Bottling
   Company
3599 Northwest Yeon Avenue
Portland, OR 97210

Douglas County Bottling
612 Northwest Cecil
Roseburg, OR 97470

Coca-Cola Bottling Company
1220 South 12th Southeast
Salem, OR 97302

Coca-Cola Bottling Company
2100 West Second
The Dalles, OR 97058

Pennsylvania

Beaver Coca-Cola Bottling
1701 Third Street
Beaver, PA 15009

Coca-Cola Bottling Company
2150 Industrial Drive
Bethlehem, PA 18001

Chambersburg Coca-Cola
  Company
Main and South Streets
Chambersburg, PA 17201

Coca-Cola Bottling Company
3 Arentzen Boulevard
Charleroi, PA 15022

Coatesville Coca-Cola Company
174 North Caln Road
Coatesville, PA 19320

Coca-Cola Bottling Company
601 East DuBois Avenue
DuBois, PA 15801

Consolidated Coca-Cola Bottling
  Company
Route 422 West
Ebensburg, PA 15931

Coca-Cola Bottling
2209 West Fiftieth Street
Erie, PA 16514

Yori's, Inc.
295 Brengle Street
Freeland, PA 18224

Greensburg Coca-Cola Bottling
501 West Otterman Street
Greensburg, PA 15601

Mid-Atlantic Canners
316 South Front Street
Hamburg, PA 19526

Mid-Atlantic Coca-Cola
1428 Manheim Pike
Lancaster, PA 17601

Coca-Cola Bottling Company
1239 West Fourth Street
Lewistown, PA 17044

Coca-Cola Bottling Company
421 North Street
Meadville, PA 16335

Coca-Cola Bottling Company
450 Delaware Avenue
Palmerton, PA 18071

Philadelphia Coca-Cola
G and Erie Avenues
Philadelphia, PA 19134

Superior Bottling Company
1-11 North Main Street
Phoenixville, PA 19460

Quaker State Coca-Cola
5722 Centre Avenue
Pittsburgh, PA 15206

Keystone Coca-Cola Bottling
300 Oak Street
Pittston, PA 18640

Glen Bottling Company
665 East Main Street
Plymouth, PA 18651

Coca-Cola Bottling Company
2200 West Market Street
Pottsville, PA 17901

Reading Coca-Cola Bottling
    Company
Bern Street and Madison Avenue
Reading, PA 19601

Coca-Cola Bottling Company
519 South Dock Street
Sharon, PA 16146

Mid-Atlantic Coca-Cola
4825 Old Gettysburg Road
Shiremanstown, PA 17011

Mid-Atlantic Coca-Cola
200 North River Avenue
Sunbury, PA 17801

Wible Bottling
Hudson Street
Three Springs, PA 17264

Endless Mountain Water Company
P.O. Box 97
Tunkhannock, PA 18657

Coca-Cola Bottling Company
244 Pittsburgh Street
Uniontown, PA 15401

Cameron Coca-Cola Bottling
    Company
124 West Maiden Street
Washington, PA 15301

Williamsport Coca-Cola Company
1350 Washington Boulevard
Williamsport, PA 17701

Coca-Cola Bottling Company
2611 East Market Street
York, PA 17402

Rhode Island
Coca-Cola Bottling Company
95 Pleasant Valley Parkway
Providence, RI 02901

South Carolina
Coca-Cola Bottling Company
208 Lane Street
Abbeville, SC 29620

Aiken Coca-Cola Bottling
621 York Street Northeast
Aiken, SC 29801

Allendale Coca-Cola Company
Railroad Avenue
Allendale, SC 29810

Coca-Cola Bottling Company
440-442 East Orr Street
Anderson, SC 29621

South Atlantic Canners
601 Cousar Street
Bishopville, SC 29010

Charleston Coca-Cola Bottling
823 Meeting Street
Charleston, SC 29402

Carolina Coca-Cola Bottling
186 Saluda Street
Chester, SC 29706

Coca-Cola Bottling Company
Highway 501 Bypass
Conway, SC 29526

Coca-Cola Bottling Company
328 South Palmetto Avenue
Denmark, SC 29042

Coastal Coca-Cola Bottling
   Company
Pisgah Road
Florence, SC 29503

Carolina Coca-Cola Bottling
113 Orange Street
Georgetown, SC 29440

Coca-Cola Bottling Company
516 Buncombe Street
Greenville, SC 29602

Greenwood Coca-Cola Bottling
311 Mineral Avenue
Greenwood, SC 29646

Hampton Bottling Works
101 Lightsey Street
Hampton, SC 29924

Carolina Coca-Cola Bottling
807 Long Street
Kingstree, SC 29556

Coca-Cola Bottling
Highway 9 Bypass
Lancaster, SC 29720

Coastal Coca-Cola Bottling
   Company
222 Railroad Avenue
Marion, SC 29571

Coca-Cola Bottling Company
Highway 601 North
Orangeburg, SC 29115

Pageland Coca-Cola Bottling
107 South Sycamore Street
Pageland, SC 29728

Rock Hill Coca-Cola
520 North Cherry Road
Rock Hill, SC 29730

Spartanburg Coca-Cola Company
500 West Main Street
Spartanburg, SC 29301

Dorchester Coca-Cola Bottling
118 South Cedar Street
Summerville, SC 29483

Carolina Coca-Cola Bottling
712 East Liberty Street
Sumter, SC 29150

Charleston Coca-Cola Bottling
1211 North Jefferies
Walterboro, SC 29488

South Dakota
Coca-Cola Bottling Company
221 North Main
Aberdeen, SD 57401

Coca-Cola Bottling Company
227 Dakota Avenue North
Huron, SD 57350

Coca-Cola Bottling Company
120 South Kimball
Mitchell, SD 57301

Coca-Cola Bottling Company
West Shore Acre
Mobridge, SD 57601

Coca-Cola Bottling Company
124 East Dakota Avenue
Pierre, SD 57501

Coca-Cola Bottling Company
837 East Saint Patrick
Rapid City, SD 57701

Coca-Cola Bottling Company
2301 South Minnesota Avenue
Sioux Falls, SD 57105

Coca-Cola Bottling Company
405 Cessna Street
Watertown, SD 57201

Tennessee
Coca-Cola Bottling Company
1303 South Dupree Street
Brownsville, TN 38012

Chattanooga Coca-Cola Company
4000 Amnicola Highway
Chattanooga, TN 37401

Coca-Cola Company
330 North Second Street
Clarksville, TN 37040

Johnston Coca-Cola Bottling
U.S. Bypass 64
Cleveland, TN 37311

Coca-Cola Bottling Company
Nashville Highway
Columbia, TN 38401

Coca-Cola Bottling Company
434 West Spring Street
Cookeville, TN 38501

Dickson Coca-Cola Bottling
    Company
101 Cowan Road
Dickson, TN 37055

Coca-Cola Bottling Company
531 East Cedar Street
Dyersburg, TN 38024

Coca-Cola Bottling Company
Highway 64-W
Fayetteville, TN 37334

Coca-Cola Bottling Company
457 Riverside Drive
Jackson, TN 38301

oca-Cola Bottling Company
10 Wesley Street
ohnson City, TN 37601

oca-Cola U.S.A.
0820 Kingston Pike
noxville, TN 37922

oddy Manufacturing Company
200 Leslie Avenue
noxville, TN 37901

oca-Cola Bottling Company
Iighway 25 West
a Follette, TN 37766

Coca-Cola Distributing
Highway 70 East
ebanon, TN 37087

Coca-Cola Bottling Company
10 Front Street
exington, TN 38351

Coca-Cola Bottling Company
199 South Hollywood Street
Memphis, TN 38111

Coca-Cola Bottling Works
510 Southeast Broad Street
Murfreesboro, TN 37130

Wometco Coca-Cola Bottling
107 Craighead Street
Nashville, TN 37204

Coca-Cola Bottling Company
611 West College Street
Pulaski, TN 38478

Johnston Coca-Cola Bottling
220 South Kingston Avenue
Rockwood, TN 37854

Coca-Cola Bottling Company
Box 408, 208 Elms
Shelbyville, TN 37160

Wometco Coca-Cola Bottling
114 North Main Street
Springfield, TN 37172

Coca-Cola Bottling Company
Manchester Highway
Tullahoma, TN 37388

Coca-Cola Bottling
1915 East Reelfoot Avenue
Union City, TN 38261

Texas

Texas Coca-Cola Bottling
    Company
2074 North First Street
Abilene, TX 79603

American Bottling Company
Sain Drive, Box 989
Alice, TX 78332

Big Bend Coca-Cola Bottling
West Highway 90
Alpine, TX 79831

Amarillo Coca-Cola Bottling
701 South Lincoln
Amarillo, TX 79105

Coca-Cola Bottling Company
9600 Burnet Road
Austin, TX 78766

Coca-Cola Bottling
1075 Mariposa
Beaumont, TX 77701

Coca-Cola Bottling
300 South Washington
Beeville, TX 78102

Texas Coca-Cola Bottling
West Highway 80
Big Spring, TX 79720

Amarillo Coca-Cola Bottling
900 Franklin Street
Borger, TX 79007

Coca-Cola Bottling Company
1301 South Horton Street
Brenham, TX 77833

Coca-Cola Bottling
1834 Los Ebanos Boulevard
Brownsville, TX 78520

Coca-Cola Bottling Company
1308 Center
Brownwood, TX 76801

Coca-Cola Bottling
201 East Twenty-Fourth Street
Bryan, TX 77806

Childress Bottling Company
200 Second Street NE
Childress, TX 79201

Coca-Cola Bottling Company
200 South Wilhite Street
Cleburne, TX 76031

Coca-Cola Bottling Company
214 South Colorado Street
Coleman, TX 76834

American Bottling Company
717 Lester
Corpus Christi, TX 78408

Coca-Cola Company
409 South Ninth
Corsicana, TX 75110

Coca-Cola Bottling Company
212 East Main Street
Cuero, TX 77954

Crossroads Canning Company
Industrial Drive
Cuero, TX 77954

Coca-Cola Bottling Company
819 Chicago
Dalhart, TX 79022

Coca-Cola Bottling Company
6011 Lemmon Avenue
Dallas, TX 75221

Shoshone Coca-Cola Bottling
1 Dallas Centre, Suite 2175
Dallas, TX 75201

Magnolia Coca-Cola Bottling
11001 Gateway West
El Paso, TX 79935

Big Bend Coca-Cola Bottling
1008 North Kansas
Fort Stockton, TX 79735

Coca-Cola Bottling Company
209 Pennsylvania
Fort Worth, TX 76104

Metro Beverage Supply
Company
5001 Northeast Parkway
Fort Worth, TX 76106

Coca-Cola Bottling
425-427 West Main Street
Fredericksburg, TX 78624

Coca-Cola Wholesale
East Highway 84
Gatesville, TX 76528

Coca-Cola Bottling Company
1040 East Fourth Street
Graham, TX 76046

Coca-Cola Bottling Company
2315-2317 Johnson Street
Greenville, TX 75401

Coca-Cola Bottling
819 North Marshall Street
Henderson, TX 75652

Amarillo Coca-Cola Bottling
529 Myrtle Street
Hereford, TX 79045

Coca-Cola Bottling Company
2800 Bissonnet
Houston, TX 77001

Crown Coca-Cola Bottling
Company
119 Nacogdoches
Jacksonville, TX 75766

Beaumont Coca-Cola Bottling
Highway 190
Jasper, TX 75951

American Bottling Company
2600 East Santa Gertrudias
Kingsville, TX 78363

Coca-Cola Bottling Company
1 Del Mar Industrial Park
Laredo, TX 78041

Beaumont Coca-Cola Bottling
1421 Main Street
Liberty, TX 77575

Coca-Cola Bottling Company
340 West Tyler Street
Longview, TX 75606

Coca-Cola Bottling Company
6101 South Avenue A
Lubbock, TX 79408

Coca-Cola Bottling Company
806 Webber
Lufkin, TX 75901

Coca-Cola Bottling
511 North Washington Street
Marshall, TX 75670

Coca-Cola Bottling
2400 Expressway
McAllen, TX 78501

Big Bend Coca-Cola Bottling
419½ Monroe
McCamey, TX 79752

McKinney Coca-Cola Bottling
800 North Chestnut Street
McKinney, TX 75069

Centex Coca-Cola Bottling
    Company
115 West Commerce
Mexia, TX 76667

Coca-Cola Bottling Company
3321 Northwest Stallings Drive
Nacogdoches, TX 75961

Permian Coca-Cola Bottling
    Company
2700 Van Street
Odessa, TX 79760

Coca-Cola Bottling Company
1515 North Hobart
Pampa, TX 79065

Coca-Cola Bottling
1033 Bonham Street
Paris, TX 75460

Big Bend Coca-Cola Bottling
1101 Pinehurst
Pecos, TX 79772

Coca-Cola Bottling
1105 Highway 15 West
Perryton, TX 79070

Caprock Canners, Inc.
300 West Fifth Street
Plainview, TX 79072

Coca-Cola Bottling
105 Highway 87 Bypass
Plainview, TX 79072

Coca-Cola Bottling Company
County Road
Port Lavaca, TX 77979

Coca-Cola Bottling Company
69 North Chadbourne
San Angelo, TX 76902

Coca-Cola Bottling
162 Exposition
San Antonio, TX 78219

Central Texas Beverage
215 West San Antonio
San Marcos, TX 78666

Permian Coca-Cola Bottling
    Company
305 Southeast Fifth Street
Seminole, TX 79360

Coca-Cola Bottling
1820 Frisco Road
Sherman, TX 75090

American Bottling Company
Highway 77 South
Sinton, TX 78387

Coca-Cola Bottling
901 East Industrial Drive
Sulphur Springs, TX 75482

Coca-Cola Bottling Company
401 North Third Street
Temple, TX 76501

Coca-Cola Bottling
1930 New Boston Road
Texarkana, TX 75501

Coca-Cola Bottling Company
3200 West Gentry Parkway
Tyler, TX 75702

Coca-Cola Bottling Company
301 South Getty
Uvalde, TX 78801

Coca-Cola Bottling Company
4002 North Navarro Street
Victoria, TX 77901

Coca-Cola Bottling Company
1201 Austin Avenue
Waco, TX 76701

Coca-Cola Bottling Company
1219 Fort Worth Street
Weatherford, TX 76086

Wichita Coca-Cola Bottling
1512 Lamar Avenue
Wichita Falls, TX 76307

Utah
Coca-Cola Bottling
151 South Main
Cedar City, UT 84720

Coca-Cola Bottling Company
975 West 800 North
Logan, UT 84321

Coca-Cola Bottling Company
2860 Pennsylvania Avenue
Ogden, UT 84402

Coca-Cola Bottling Company
Route 2, Box 7B
Price, UT 84501

Coca-Cola Bottling Company
825 South 200 West
Provo, UT 84601

Coca-Cola Bottling
146 South Main
Richfield, UT 84701

Coca-Cola Bottling Company
875 Southwest Temple
Salt Lake City, UT 84104

Coca-Cola Bottling Company
800 North Vernal Avenue
Vernal, UT 84078

Vermont
Coca-Cola Bottling Company
Route 14
Barre, VT 05641

Coca-Cola Bottling Company
Vermont Meadows Interstate 89
Colchester, VT 05446

Coca-Cola Bottling Company
Quality Lane
Rutland, VT 05701

Mid-Atlantic Coca-Cola Company
Route 13
Exmore, VA 23350

Mid-Atlantic Coca-Cola Company
2011 Princess Ann Street
Fredericksburg, VA 22401

Virginia

Mid-Atlantic Coca-Cola Company
5401 Seminary Road
Alexandria, VA 22313

Wometco Coca-Cola Bottling
Blue Ridge Avenue
Bedford, VA 24523

Dixie Coca-Cola Bottling
Company
1913-1935 West State Street
Bristol, VA 24201

Central Coca-Cola Bottling
Company
722 Preston Avenue
Charlottesville, VA 22901

Roanoke Coca-Cola Bottling
Company
720 Main Street
Clifton Forge, VA 24422

Wometco Coca-Cola Bottling
U.S. Highway 100 South
Dublin, VA 24084

Emporia Coca-Cola Bottling
Company
518 Halifax Street
Emporia, VA 23847

Wometco Coca-Cola Bottling
Company
Roseland Road
Galax, VA 24333

Coca-Cola Bottling
Main Street
Gloucester, VA 23061

Coca-Cola Bottling
794 North Main Street
Harrisonburg, VA 22801

Wometco Coca-Cola Bottling
Company
229 West Nelson Street
Lexington, VA 24450

Coca-Cola Bottling
3720 Cohen Place
Lynchburg, VA 24506

Coca-Cola Bottling Company
P.O. Box 123
Marion, VA 24354

Contract Canners
1220 South Memorial Avenue
Martinsville, VA 24112

Mid-Atlantic Coca-Cola
1710 Goodridge Drive
Mc Lean, VA 22102

Northern Neck Coca-Cola
Kings Highway and Rectory Road
Montross, VA 22520

Mid-Atlantic Coca-Cola Company
3000 Monticello Avenue
Norfolk, VA 23517

Lonesome Pine Coca-Cola
813 Sixth Avenue
Norton, VA 24273

Central Coca-Cola Bottling
  Company
1706 Roseneath Road
Richmond, VA 23230

Wometco Coca-Cola Bottling
340-346 Center Avenue NW
Roanoke, VA 24033

Coca-Cola Bottling Company
Riverside Drive
St. Paul, VA 24283

Coca-Cola Bottling Company
Highway 58 West
South Boston, VA 24592

Central Coca-Cola Bottling
  Company
Road 647, Route 11 South
Staunton, VA 24401

Mid-Atlantic Coca-Cola Company
1390 Progress Road
Suffolk, VA 23434

Lonesome Pine Coca-Cola
P.O. Box 9
Vansant, VA 24656

Mid-Atlantic Coca-Cola Company
U.S. Route 211-29 North
Warrenton, VA 22186

Dixie Coca-Cola Warehouse
P.O. Box 212
Weber City, VA 24251

Central Coca-Cola Bottling
  Company
1720 Valley Avenue
Winchester, VA 22601

Washington

Pacific Coca-Cola Bottling
  Company
1150 124th Avenue Northeast
Bellevue, WA 98005

Coca-Cola Bottling Company
2101 Woburn Street
Bellingham, WA 98226

Pacific Coca-Cola Bottling
  Company
7610 47th Avenue Northeast
Marysville, WA 98270

Coca-Cola Bottling Company
1740 Pheasant Avenue
Moses Lake, WA 98837

Pacific Coca-Cola Bottling
123 North Main Street
Omak, WA 98841

Coca-Cola Bottling Company
730 East Front Street
Port Angeles, WA 98362

Anchorage Cold Storage Company
26 South Hanford
Seattle, WA 98134

Pacific Coca-Cola Bottling
  Company
North 901 Monroe
Spokane, WA 99201

Pacific Coca-Cola Bottling
  Company
3333 South 38th Street
Tacoma, WA 98409

Coca-Cola Bottling Company
928 West Main, Box 794
Walla Walla, WA 99362

Coca-Cola Bottling Company
16-20 North Columbia Street
Wenatchee, WA 98801

Coca-Cola Bottling Company
113 South Sixth Avenue
Yakima, WA 98902

Coca-Cola Bottling Tri-Cities
P.O. Box 2405
Pasco, WA 99301

West Virginia
Wometco Coca-Cola Bottling
  Company
700 South Oakwood Avenue
Beckley, WV 25801

Northfork Coca-Cola Bottling
Route 5, Penical View Road
Bluefield, WV 24701

Coca-Cola Bottling Company
3211 MacCorkle Avenue SE
Charleston, WV 25304

Wellslee Coca-Cola Bottling
P.O. Box 186
Craigsville, WV 26205

Coca-Cola Bottling
Eleventh and Davis Avenue
Elkins, WV 26241

Central Coca-Cola Bottling
1200 Morgantown Avenue
Fairmont, WV 26554

Coca-Cola Bottling Company
401 Third Avenue
Huntington, WV 25701

Coca-Cola Bottling Company
P.O. Box 360
Logan, WV 25601

Coca-Cola Bottling Company
518 Third Avenue
Marlinton, WV 24954

Wellslee Coca-Cola Bottling
Lawless Road
Morgantown, WV 26505

Coca-Cola Bottling Company
1600 Thirteenth Street
Parkersburg, WV 26101

Wometco Coca-Cola Bottling
Company
Box 434
Pineville, WV 24874

Central Coca-Cola Bottling
Company
126 East Main Street
Romney, WV 26757

Cameron Coca-Cola Bottling
Company
225 Burt Street
Sisterville, WV 26175

Northfork Coca-Cola Bottling
Virginia Avenue
Welch, WV 24801

Wisconsin
Coca-Cola Bottling Company
1137 Elm Street
Antigo, WI 54409

Mid-West Coca-Cola Bottling
1800 West Front Street
Ashland, WI 54806

Coca-Cola Bottling Company
520 East Burnett Street
Beaver Dam, WI 53916

Coca-Cola Bottling Company
623 Hastings Way
Eau Claire, WI 54701

Ellsworth Bottling Works
410 Wall Street
Ellsworth, WI 54010

Coca-Cola Bottling Company
2523 South Oneida Street
Green Bay, WI 54304

Coca-Cola Bottling Company
1107 West Avalon Road
Janesville, WI 53545

Coca-Cola Bottling Company
5017 Sheridan Road
Kenosha, WI 53140

Coca-Cola Bottling Company
1630 Miller Street
LaCrosse, WI 54601

Sheridan Springs Coca-Cola
Sheridan Springs Road
Lake Geneva, WI 53147

Coca-Cola Bottling Company
3536 University Avenue
Madison, WI 53705

Coca-Cola Bottling Company
1740 Industrial Parkway
Marinette, WI 54143

Coca-Cola Bottling Company
2727 West Silver Spring
Milwaukee, WI 53209

Coca-Cola Bottling Company
1404 South Main Street
Oshkosh, WI 54903

Coca-Cola Bottling
County Highway H
Phillips, WI 54555

Coca-Cola Bottling Company
902 Plover Road
Plover, WI 54467

Coca-Cola Bottling Company
1415 Iverson Street
Rhinelander, WI 54501

Rice Lake Coca-Cola Bottling
326 South Main
Rice Lake, WI 54868

Jensen Distributing Company
250 Summit Street
River Falls, WI 54022

Coca-Cola Bottling Company
Highway 29 East
Shawano, WI 54166

Coca-Cola Bottling Company
1837 North Avenue
Sheboygan, WI 53081

Coca-Cola Bottling Company
1930 Grand Avenue
Wausau, WI 54401

Wisconsin Dells Coca-Cola
919 Bowman Road
Wisconsin Dells, WI 53965

Big Horn Coca-Cola Bottling
1462 Rumsey Street
Cody, WY 82414

Rawlins Distributing Company
104 Eighth Street
Rawlins, WY 82301

Coca-Cola Company
P.O. Box 939
Rock Springs, WY 82901

Wy-Mont Beverages
200 Paul Street
Sheridan, WY 82801

Wyoming
Coca-Cola Bottling Company
401 East Fifteenth Street
Cheyenne, WY 82001

Index

About the author

Coca-Cola memorabilia was as much a part of Deborah Goldstein Hill's childhood as slumber parties and high school proms. However, she became even more involved with Coca-Cola memorabilia when she took over her father's publishing business in 1979. Because of the demand for *Coca-Cola Collectibles, Volumes I-IV,* she began reprinting the books immediately. She also put together an *Index* to the four volumes for easier access and current pricing.

Deborah has corresponded with thousands of collectors over the years, written a column for more than a year, and traveled to many swapmeets and auctions. This book is the culmination of her experiences with and knowledge of Coca-Cola memorabilia.

She welcomes your correspondence and appreciates your continuing interest in Coca-Cola collectibles.